The

LOIRE VALLEY

The

LOIRE VALLEY

Plantagenet & Valois

by

HENRY MYHILL

with an appendix on the wines

by

GEORGE MORTIMER

London FABER AND FABER *Boston*

PUBLISHER'S NOTE

Sadly, Henry Myhill died suddenly in Algiers in April 1977 shortly after finishing the manuscript of this book. Thanks are due to Ralph Hancock for preparing the manuscript for the printer.

First published in 1978
by Faber and Faber Limited
3 Queen Square London WC1
Printed in Great Britain by
Western Printing Services Ltd
Bristol
All rights reserved
© *1978 the estate of Henry Myhill*

British Library Cataloguing in
Publication Data
Myhill, Henry
 The Loire Valley
 1. Loire valley – Description
 and travel   I. Title
 914.4'5'0483   DC611.L81
 ISBN 0-571-10446-0

Contents

Appendices

Illustrations   *following page* 64

To

FRANK HERRMANN

in whose company
I first visited the Loire Valley

Introduction

Before this book can be written I must project myself into the future and ask why it is in your hands.

Perhaps you have decided to spend a holiday, or even just part of a holiday, in the Loire Valley. Perhaps you want to know more about that particular part of France, without any immediate intention of visiting it. Or perhaps, as you strolled along the shelves of your public library, the title itself aroused your interest. Certainly those are my own three reasons for reading travel books and guides.

So putting myself in your place, I must try to supply the information you seek in a way you will find acceptable. The necessary facts and background must be given, but not in indigestible detail. Much that is less essential will deliberately be omitted. Prices, naturally, which in this inflationary age are out of date before they are printed. The hours and the months when châteaux and museums are open, and the days when they are closed, for these too change from year to year. They are also readily available in that excellent free guide *Val de Loire – pays des châteaux*, supplied by the French Government Tourist Office in London, or by the local Syndicats d'Initiative of the Régions of the Centre and of the Pays de la Loire which have combined to publish it.

But I may also have little to say about many charming but minor monuments. Nor shall I dwell at inordinate length on every aspect of even the major ones. For I am acutely aware that this is not the first book about the Loire, and that in trying to follow exactly the same plan as a long succession of previous writers I would be inviting unfavourable comparisons. Freda White, who initiated this series of books about France with three guides which will never be equalled, refused ever to touch the Loire, which she felt had been treated by too many writers already.

Two further reasons cause me to avoid their more obvious, sometimes almost poetic approach. The first is that one purpose of this book is to fill the gap between the areas covered in Freda White's *Ways of Aquitaine* and my own book *Brittany*, but not far enough north to constitute part of Normandy.

This gap does not correspond exactly with the 'classic' Loire Valley from Gien to Angers, with its necklace of châteaux which are household words the world over. Still less does it correspond with the Loire Valley along its entire length from its source on the distant Gerbier de Jonc all the way to the Atlantic. For its upper course through the Massif Central, where it is almost a different species of river, has already been covered by Freda White in *West of the Rhône*; while I have described its lower reaches and estuary in *Brittany*.

On the other hand the 'gap' includes a wide area to the north, up to the limits of the ancient counties of Anjou and Maine, which is largely unknown to English-speaking visitors, and which receives little mention in the usual guides. This area has rightly been placed in the modern administrative region of the Pays de la Loire, for it shares a common climate and a common history with the great unruly river towards which flow its own more placid streams. But extending the range of the guide to cover this area is already to force it out of the classic mould.

This brings me to my second reason for wishing to avoid this mould. Because the major monuments of the classic Loire Valley were built by an aristocratic élite, it has appealed to writers profoundly in sympathy with that élite if not actually members of it. So great has been their identification that they have looked at the countryside they were describing with the very eyes of Charles VIII or of François I. Rivers they have seen simply as waterways for pleasure barges, or as providing a pleasing prospect. Fields exist to be trimmed into parkland, or flattened into formal gardens. Forests are for hunting.

Now this writer belongs to no élite, aristocratic or otherwise. He can therefore enjoy this region objectively, as it is today, without mistaken nostalgia for a grandiose past. But note that he intends to enjoy it. Although objective, the view presented will not be that of the professional economist or sociologist, thick with statistics.

This is the easier because there exists an alternative to the aristocratic approach. For the Loire Valley has not only provided a background, a stage set as it were, for royal masques, for hunting parties, and for lordly architectural whims. It has also provided, from its very soil, the three writers who incarnate the French spirit more truly than the builders of Chambord and Chenonceaux, Amboise and Azay-le-Rideau.

That proud citizen of Tours, the historian Pierre Levéel, has written of 'the so valued balance of the Tourangeau character – Rabelais corrected by Descartes'. The mocking, full-blooded, life-loving Rabelaisian spirit requires no more explanation than the rational, analytical Cartesian, for both have entered this language as well as their own. In any case there will be more to say about these writers in connection with the places with which they are associated.

The third member of this trinity is Charles Péguy. He is less well known than the others, he represents an even deeper aspect of the French spirit. For beneath the emotion so evident in Rabelais, beneath even the reason represented by Descartes, lies faith.

His was a very special faith, a refined Catholicism tempered by a peculiarly pure patriotism. Outside literature its greatest exponent is Joan of Arc, whose own career reached its highest moments beside the Loire. It is therefore not surprising that Charles Péguy felt an affinity with her. Indeed his early *Le Mystère de la Charité de Jeanne d'Arc* was written long before his idealistic socialism had been transmuted and enriched by his religious conversion.

His own childhood on the outskirts of Orléans was a good deal poorer than that of Rabelais or of Descartes, both of whom came from professional backgrounds. But the families of all three belonged to the region, and drew their living directly from it. They saw the great châteaux as we do, as standing for a way of life quite apart from their own. Indeed even more than us they could recognise them as existing in an ideal world, superimposed from afar on the rural realities of the Loire Valley.

It can therefore be claimed that this region is the cultural heart of France on two distinct levels: that of its tolerant, clear-thinking, patriotic sons; and that of a sophisticated, aristocratic, ruling élite which at one period chose to reside there. To this claim is often added a geographical argument: that the Loire is more central in France than the Seine.

From this it is but a short step to asserting that one of its cities would more suitably have fulfilled the role of capital than Paris, within all too easy reach of the northern frontier. The best French, moreover, one is so often told, is not Parisian, but *tourangeau*.

This geographical argument can be pushed too far. The Loire may be longer than the Seine, but it is very much less navigable. Paris may be too far north, but Tours, the city of the Loire most frequently put forward as a replacement, is certainly too far west.

And in Touraine, the countryfolk, at least, adopt a deprecating manner whenever one suggests that they are the repositories of the purest French. 'I suppose it's true that we make fewer mistakes than some of our neighbours' is the nearest they will come to accepting your compliment.

While amongst those neighbours, both to west and to east, dialect lives on. Works are still published in *angevin* patois. *Chansonniers* in Belle-Epoque Paris kept their audiences in fits by adopting a crude *beauceron* accent and vocabulary, just as Molière's peasants had done two and a half centuries earlier.

The Beauce, where this is spoken, is the immense, corn-covered plateau stretching south from Paris and only broken, barely ten miles from the Loire, by the Forest of Orléans. At its western limit stands Chartres, in whose cathedral Gothic architecture and the stained-glass window receive their most triumphant expression. The presence of its two spires, even when invisible, dominates those vast green or yellow fields all the way to Etampes and Rambouillet. Crossing them, we understand why Charles Péguy entitled his finest, noblest poem *La présentation de la Beauce à Notre Dame de Chartres*.

But for most of the journey those spires are out of sight. For the Beauce, despite first appearances, is far from flat. On the particular route followed on foot by Péguy, when twice he made a private pilgrimage from Paris, they only appear, suddenly and dramatically above the horizon, as one breasts a slight rise a mere eleven miles away.

Until I came to follow his route I had regarded Chartres as belonging to the outer Paris suburbs. This is understandable, for when driving one has soon swept through, or rather past it, on one's way further west. But approached at greater leisure it remains a tiny urban island in a rural ocean. And entering it by the very path he took; between gardens, across a tiny bridge over a scarcely flowing Eure, and up the steep hill where the plaque bearing his bust has appropriately been fixed, it seems as much of a quiet country town as it must have done to him just before the First World War.

Nor is Chartres just an 'identikit' country town which might be anywhere. It is a country town which already belongs to the West – just as there are corners of north-east Hampshire, and even of Surrey, only a few miles out of London, which in speech and atmosphere already hint at the West Country. This book will not deal with it in detail, for the infant Eure on which it lies runs off north to join the Seine. But a halt there is not only an architectural experience in itself, but also a useful mental preparation on the way to the Loire Valley.

To belong to l'Ouest is not for everyone the height of praise. Richard Cobb, the most penetrating historian writing on France today, whose knowledge of the land is so profound and so personal that he called his autobiographical essay *A Second Identity*, has some hard things to say about the deadness of Western France, and about the untypically French lack of intellectual sparkle he has found in Tours in particular. It is true that he has personal reasons for reacting a little sharply against the traditional images of Touraine as the province of kings, and of *le juste milieu*.

One is obliged neither to accept his view entirely, nor to reject it out of hand. The bucolic, 'West Country' aspect of the Loire Valley need not displace these other two. It can be added to them. And it will be useful to bear in mind after moving away from the great river into those poorer, less fertile regions which feed it, but which were hardly noticed by Rabelais, Ronsard, or Chrétien de Troyes, or by their royal masters, Plantagenet and Valois.

H.M.   *January 1977*

The

LANDSCAPE

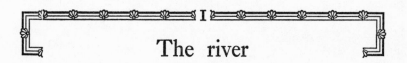

The river

All great rivers transform the countryside through which they flow. But in general, they themselves are a necessary part of that country-side. Their presence is due to the effect of geological accident on a particular area of the earth's surface.

Thus the structure of North and South America made inevitable the existence of the Mississippi and of the Amazon. Similarly, the structure of Europe determined the existence and the course of four of the five great rivers that flow through France: the Rhône, the Rhine, the Garonne, and the Seine.

Only the upper course of the Loire – not the part with which this guide is concerned – was formed in this way. And for many millions of years that was all the Loire there was: a swift mountain stream whose waters joined the Seine near Moret, only forty-five miles upstream from Paris. Had it continued to follow this course, it would not today be one of France's five great rivers.

This is not only because it would have been shorter, narrower, and less powerful. For 'great river' is an imprecise and inadequate translation of the French word *fleuve*. The essential characteristic of a *fleuve* is that it flows into the sea. Any other course of water, how-ever large, is known as a *rivière*.

In fact, many *rivières* are longer and more powerful than many *fleuves*. But such shorter *fleuves*, draining only a restricted basin, are classed simply as *fleuves côtiers* (coastal). Only a large river which reaches the sea is a *fleuve* without qualification.

The Loire is certainly large. But it is not a great waterway, a river highway, like most *fleuves*. Although it has borne plenty of traffic in the past, this always faced problems, and quickly vanished with the coming of the railway. The reason for this is the irregularity

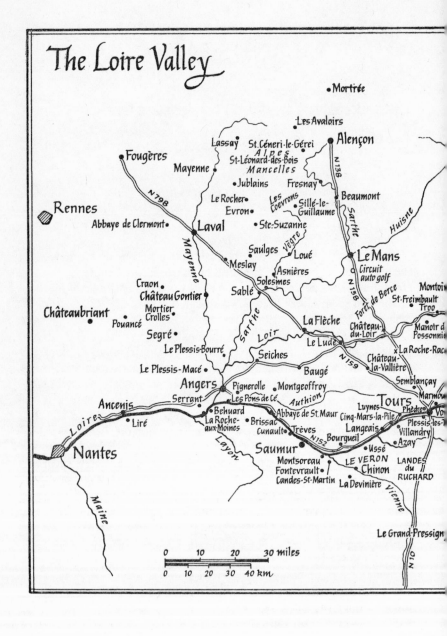

The Loire Valley

Mortrée

Les Avaloirs

Lassay   St.Céneri-le-Gérei   Alençon

Fougères   *Alpes*
Mayenne   St-Léonard-des-Bois   *Mancelles*   Beaumont

Jublains   Fresnay

Rennes   Le Rocher   Les   Sillé-le-
Abbaye de Clermont   Evron   *Coevrons*   Guillaume

Laval   Ste-Suzanne   Le Mans

Saulges   *Vègre*   Loué   Circuit
auto golf

Craon   Meslay   Asnières
Château Gontier   Solesmes   *Forêt de Bercé*   Montoi
Châteaubriant   Mortier   Sablé   St-Freimbault
Crolles   Troo

Pouancé   La Flèche   Manoir d
Segré   Château-   Possonni
Le Plessis-Bourré   *Loir*   du-Loir

Le Lude   x La Roche-Rac
Seiches   Château-
Le Plessis-Macé   la-Vallière

Baugé   Semblançay
Angers   Pignerolle   Montgeoffroy   Marmou
Ancenis   Serrant   Les Pons de Cé   *Authion*   Tours
Béhuard   Abbaye de St. Maur   Luynes   Vo
Liré   La Roche-   Brissac   Cinq-Mars-la-Pile   Phèdr
aux-Moines   Cunault   Trèves   Langeais   Plessis-les-
Nantes   Saumur   Bourgueil   Villandry
Azay
Montsoreau   Ussé   LE VERON   LANDES
Fontevrault   Chinon   du
Candes-St-Martin   La Devinière   RUCHARD

Le Grand-Pressign

0   10   20   30 miles
0   10   20   30   40 km

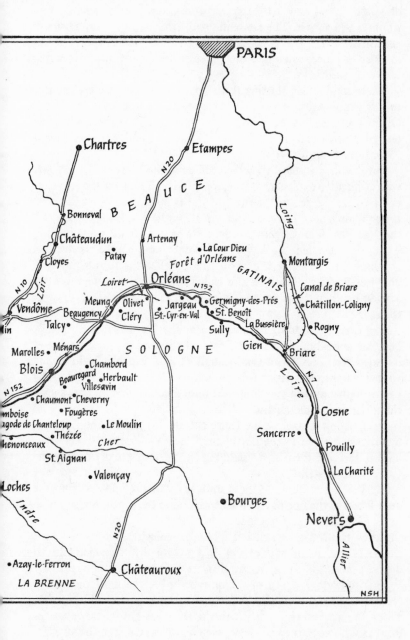

of its flow: full and fast in spring and autumn, light and slow in summer and winter. The Loire in flood, sweeping against its bridges and threatening its dykes, has up to three hundred times its power in a dry summer, when it lapses into a string of streams meandering between sandbanks.

These sandbanks, shifting from season to season, were a menace to navigation even in the broader stretches below Orléans. Above Orléans traffic was generally only one-way. The boats or rafts floated downstream from the Massif Central, and were afterwards there broken up for wood.

But this very instability, which rendered the Loire navigable only with difficulty, explains its transforming role. During the Tertiary era a relatively gentle lowering of the continent towards the west brought an arm of the sea as far inland as Blois. Geologists call this the Mer des Faluns, from the deposits of tiny shells it left behind. This slight tilt led the Loire to follow a new course. Instead of continuing to flow north beyond Briare, where its former valley is now followed by a small stream called the Loing, it turned to form a wide bend, north-west to Orléans and then south-west towards the sea.

The first region to be transformed by the Loire as it cut this new bed was one which it had itself created at an even earlier period of its existence. This was a vast triangle of land which it had covered with incompletely broken-down débris. This was not properly broken down and so was infertile; until a century ago it was something between a marsh and a desert.

In changing its course the Loire cut off this region, the Sologne, from its extension to the north, the Forest of Orléans. Today it is hard to imagine them as a single region, for they are divided by the Loire Valley itself.

'Le Val' is the name of these middle reaches. It differs from the poor forest to the north, and the heathland to the south, not so much in its altitude – the difference of level is small – as in the soil. By the time the Loire turned left it was no longer the torrent which covered the Sologne with gravel. It now brought down rich alluvial deposits from the Massif Central in its spring and autumn floods.

This fertile soil, the *limon*, continues to be the most distinctive feature of the Val even after it becomes more of a real valley, further west. The ground through which the river has cut its way changes from sand to clay, then to chalk, as older layers come to the surface.

Finally, just beyond Angers, it breaks through the barrier of pre-Cambrian granite to enter the ancient, eroded Armorican *massif* of Brittany.

But although the hinterland of the valley alters with this succession of changes, the Val itself changes little from province to province, except to become wider and more intensely cultivated.

This cultivation, due to the covering of rich alluvial soil, contrasts sharply with that of the countryside both to north and south. During its great 'bend' the Loire is a green ribbon running alongside a marshy heath. Below Orléans it runs between dry plateaux.

Some of these plateaux are covered with great forests which reach far to the south of the river: the forests of Chambord, of Amboise, or of Chinon, for example, which provided the royal families with hunting. To the north they are more frequently bare, though modern farming techniques have now made them more productive.

The term for these almost deserted uplands is *gâtines*. Surprisingly they cover most of Touraine, the so-called 'garden of France'.

If the Loire had not taken its present course, widening its valley with its twice-yearly floods, and covering it with rich soil, the *gâtines* would have been even more extensive. For although its main tributaries, the Cher, the Indre, the Vienne and the Maine, are large rivers in their own right, they are not enough to transform the landscape of several provinces.

If the Loire had been more regular in its flow, it might have been a great artery of commerce. But it would have had less effect on its surroundings.

The landscape thus formed dominates the region, rather than the *rivières*, *gâtines* and *bocage* which make up its greater part. The Loire Valley has an image of its own. Visitors know what to expect before they even get there: Rabelais and François I; good wine and beautiful women; medieval pageantry and Renaissance art; and all the carefully-tended pleasure gardens and rich orchards associated with them. The climate is almost Mediterranean, and the light – that of a Quattrocento canvas – increases the Italianate impression.

As a result, it is easy to overlook the more featureless lands crossed on the way there: the flat, bare cornlands of the Beauce; the chalky uplands and sparse pine plantations of the *gâtines*, the peaceful countryside of Maine, and notice only the château-dominated riverscape which includes formal *parterres*, vineyards, and villages of ancient, crumbling stone.

This view fulfils all expectations; even the climate and the quality of light are appropriate to landscape, vegetation and monuments. Autumn here remains mellow after winter has come to other regions more to the south and no further from the sea. The space across which immense clouds hang almost motionless above the Loire is less a sky than a firmament.

Again this is due to the river itself, carving out a wide corridor up which the temperate air masses from the Atlantic can modify the climate and atmosphere for hundreds of miles inland. But it has not always acted alone in transforming the landscape through which it flows, for it has had much help from man.

Few landscapes are so obviously, even self-consciously, civilised. But human agency is responsible not only for vines, villages, churches and châteaux. It has acted here in a less apparent, and in some respects in a less beneficial way.

Attempts were made to render the Loire navigable as early as the fifteenth century: the merchants of the towns bordering the river persuaded the kings to start raising the banks to control its flow. The Valois' personal presence on the Loire, first by necessity when they had nowhere else to go, and later by choice, made them ready to listen.

The purpose of these *levées* or dykes, greatly extended by Henri IV and in later times, was to canalise and deepen such water as remained in the wide bed during the summer drought. But they also canalised the floods, so that only a few hours separate a rise in the water at Nevers from its arrival down-river at Orléans.

This canalisation deprived the valley of the annual renewal of soil to which it owed its fertility. Although it has remained fertile, and during the past century it has been possible to replace many of the deficiencies which developed, the middle Loire remains garden-like in spite of, rather than because of the river having been brought under control.

The control has not always been complete. Several high floods in the nineteenth century, then in 1910, and again as recently as 1944, have broken through the defences. Although these have been continually raised and strengthened, they cannot be absolutely guaranteed to withstand another exceptional flood. They did not even altogether succeed in their main purpose of making the Loire navigable; but they in themselves provided an alternative. The top of the *levées* formed a direct, all-weather route, still followed by the main roads of today.

For this reason the Route Nationale 152, which follows the right bank, is frustrating to drive along. Its enforced constriction makes it narrow, with space for barely two lanes. Bending this way and that with the river, it offers few uninterrupted stretches where a line of traffic can overtake a slow-moving vehicle. For the driver at least, most of the scenic advantages provided by the *levée* are therefore illusory. For other observers too, a stretch of water, however beautiful, suffers when seen amid the din of engines and the fumes from exhausts.

There are two alternative methods of getting close to the river, and of seeing it as it should be seen, in tranquillity. The simplest is to watch carefully, on the Michelin map and on the signposts, for the stretches where the *levée* runs some distance from the bank, or where the road runs inland to take a short cut. Sometimes on such stretches a narrow road branches off from the highway, to a hamlet at the water's edge – as at Cour-sur-Loire between Mer and Ménars. Elsewhere, lanes pointing towards 'La Loire' will lead down a secluded *impasse* to where a couple of flat-bottomed and waterlogged boats, apparently neglected, lie in a tiny creek.

The other method is to take to one of these boats, or better to a canoe. This is what the writer Arthur Koestler did for his summer holiday in 1956. Some idea of his speed, and of the energy he expended, came out in the title he gave the article in which he described this: 'Drifting on a river'.* In two weeks, with a little gentle paddling, the current itself carried him at the rate of twenty miles a day all the way from Nevers down to Saumur.

'Drifting' is an attitude of mind as much as a form of inactivity. For Koestler the hazards which make the Loire unnavigable became diversions in the day's drift: sandbanks to rest against, islands to be explored, stone bridges to be negotiated, shallows round which the canoe must be portaged.

This attitude of mind, induced by the experience itself, was the right one in which to see the buildings along the Loire as they were built to be seen. Before the roads existed, the river, with all its deficiencies, formed the most frequent approach to them. And many châteaux – Sully or Amboise, for example – not only included the

---

* First published in the *Observer*, August 1957, and republished in his collection of essays, *Drinkers of Infinity*, Hutchinson, 1968.

river in their design, but were designed to be arrived at by water.
To quote Koestler:

> 'A château on the Loire, visited during a short stop in passing, is
> like a quotation out of context... It was peak tourist season in one
> of the most tourist-haunted regions of the world, but all along the
> Royal Valley we had the river to ourselves. It gave one a wonder-
> fully smug feeling of superiority to drift slowly past the turrets of
> Chaumont or Amboise, alone and unseen – like walking along the
> corridors of the Louvre after closing-time; to watch them at first
> from a distance, transparent, white and unreal, slowly growing,
> vanishing round a bend, bursting into view again unexpectedly
> huge and forbidding; and to see them all the time from the river
> which they were built to dominate; which was their *raison d'être*.'

Few may follow Koestler in what he calls *le canotage gastro-
nomique*. But whatever the means of transport, take the trouble to
get close to the river which has transformed this diverse region and
given it unity. As he says, 'a few miles from bustling towns like
Orléans . . . you are in a sunny, silent wilderness where a dog's bark
is an event and the rustling of the current against a dead branch
sounds like the Niagara Falls'. At such moments 'this, one realises
with a sudden shock, is essential France, a landscape written in
basic French, glimpsed through the back door of a deserted waterway'.

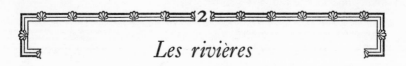

2

Les rivières

Any river which does not reach the sea is not a *fleuve*, but a *rivière*.
This word describes every waterway in the region except the Loire
itself. Many of these are substantial. One tributary, the Allier, is at
many seasons bigger than the main stream when they merge just
below Nevers. But they all lack the hidden power which one senses
in the Loire even when its waters are lowest.

What they lose in scale, however, they gain in intimacy – a necessary constituent of affection. Ask anyone who knows the region to describe the landscape conjured up for them by the words 'Pays de la Loire'. You will find that the picture in their mind's eye invariably includes a river. But for most of them this river will not be the Loire. It will be the Loiret, the Cher, the Indre, the Vienne, the Loir, the Sarthe, the Mayenne, or even some smaller stream, itself a tributary of one of these tributaries.

This is because it is easier to feel at home with waterways which are less wide and more predictable. I remember the shock on learning that the River of *The Wind in the Willows* was the Thames Kenneth Grahame knew at Cookham. I had seen the doings of Rat and Mole and Otter against an imaginary but much more intimate background: one that I was only to recognise many years later, in the Maine. This river is so still that it hardly seems to flow. Even in high summer, it laps up against its banks without leaving a slimy mudbank below high watermark. There is no risk of serious flooding, for the flat banks are almost on a level with the water.

On the bank sits an angler. Hereabouts he generally wears a peaked cap or a shapeless felt hat rather than a beret. He sits as still as the water, and seems as much a part of the landscape as the old stone bridge a couple of hundred yards upstream, or the grey stone cottages and ancient church just visible beyond.

A couple of flat-bottomed punts are moored to the bank, just as they would be on the Loire itself. But here, within these smaller horizons, they seem to have a more useful role to play.

What this scene shares with one on the Loire itself is the sky: its immensity, the quality of its all-pervading light, the great opalescent clouds hanging from it are the same. The valleys of these tributaries carry the climate of the Vallée de la Loire over the entire region.

The biggest of these tributaries, the Cher, the Indre and the Vienne, enter the Loire from its left bank. They are so large that some of their tributaries, too, are important rivers in their own right. The three biggest of these: the Loir, the Sarthe and the Mayenne, are technically tributaries of the Maine. This runs a mere five miles from where they merge to where it too merges with the Loire. As part of the same confusion Angers, really a city of the Loire, lies in fact on the Maine. Yet the old province of Maine was quite different from the old province of Anjou.

The explanation is that Mayenne is simply a deformation of

Maine, the region through which the Mayenne flows, and to which it gave its earlier name.

The Loir, as its name suggests, has much in common with the Loire. It flows past châteaux, impressive in their perfection, or even more so in their ruins, past small towns and villages, cave dwellings in the white tufa more elaborate than those of the Loire itself. But few of those châteaux have a comparable grandeur, and the forests, always held at arm's length by the unpredictable Loire, approach far closer to the banks of the Loir.

This simple, rural quality is still more marked in the Sarthe and the Mayenne. Each of these has given its name to a *département*, and the names have taken root, almost effacing the memory of the ancient province of Maine, of which they were once a part.

This is significant. To the average Frenchman, Calvados or Côtes-du-Nord are not immediately recognisable as *départements* of Normandy and Brittany. Yet Normandy and Brittany – and Burgundy and Touraine, Anjou and Poitou – still evoke distinct images, nearly two centuries after they were officially erased from the map.

Maine is one of the very few provinces which has almost completely disappeared from the popular imagination. Yet unlike Béarn or Saintonge, for example, which are still remembered, despite their having to share a *préfecture* with other old provinces, Maine's ancient limits correspond almost exactly with those of its two successors.

One reason for this may be that the slow-flowing Sarthe and Mayenne have a strong affinity with the gentle countryside through which they wind, and which bears their name. Although no one would describe them as of dramatic tourist appeal, surprisingly large numbers of people spend their holidays there. An article in a French magazine about 'a typical village' or 'the unspoilt rural heart of France', seems invariably to deal with the Sarthe.

In the same way Maine may well be chosen as the setting of a rural story, simply because it inspires so little regional loyalty. The writer on Brittany, or the poet who sings of Provence, is automatically regarded as *particulariste*, as *régionaliste*, or even as *nationaliste*. A feature or photograph describing Maine, on the other hand, celebrates the entire French countryside.

A majority of Frenchmen, with much greater reason than their English contemporaries, still regard themselves as countrymen at heart. The real industrialisation of France has only taken place since 1945. Millions of city-dwellers have once lived in the country, or are at most only one generation away from the leisurely existence which finds its expression in the unhurried *rivières* of the Pays de la Loire.

Gâtine

Gâtine is what the Loire Valley would have been without the river, or at least without the lower part of the *rivières*, cutting through these bare plateaux. Michelet likened them to 'a homespun cloak with golden fringes'. The comparison strikes the visitor, unprepared for these poor uplands, empty heaths and immense forests as soon as he leaves the narrow limits of the 'Garden of France'.

If it were not for the *rivières*, those limits would be narrower still. Less than two miles separate the Forêt de Blois on the right bank from the forests on the left which were once hunted from Chambord and still are from Cheverny. The fertile band would be just as narrow throughout Touraine and Anjou but for the widening effect of these tributaries. In particular the Cher and the Indre to the left, and the Cisse and the Authion to the right, take it in turns to run parallel to the river for many miles before finally joining it. Even so, the sparse woods of the Gâtine de Touraine are separated across the Loire and the Indre together by a mere three miles from the Forest of Chinon, and by a distance only slightly greater from the sheep pastures of the Champeigne Tourangelle.

The word *champagne*, of which *champeigne* is another form, has a rich sound to English ears. But it is only a variant of *campagne*, in its sense of open countryside, without hedges or other divisions. The open fields of the mediaeval village were unobstructed in this way, and hence *campagne* was increasingly used to describe country-side in general. One *champagne*, larger than the others, gave its name to a province, and so to the sparkling wine it produced. But there are others scattered over northern France. The *gâtines* above the Loire, where they are not forested, are all *champagnes* in this sense. Over the past century and a half their soil has been enriched by the addition of lime and fertilisers. But this increase in yield has come too late to alter the long-established pattern of settlement. Towns are little more than villages, and villages are merely hamlets. Between them the vast fields are interrupted only by the occasional fortress-like farm, whose stark walls, often showing a windowless front to the road, seem quite apart from the nearby Val.

Solitude has its own appeal. Combined with the great royal hunting forests to the south of the river, and the more recently-planted pinewoods to the north, with their lonely lakes, the *gâtine* has additional charm for the visitor to this region.

It is a charm more apparent to someone with time to spare. He will enjoy staying in its meagre townships: Noyant or Château-la-Vallière or Ste-Maure, soon left behind on walks into the empty countryside, and only coming to life on market day.

The monuments, though attractive, are thinner on the ground than in the Valley, and generally belong to an earlier period. The châteaux are often still *châteaux-forts*, real castles rather than country houses. Among the more important monuments are the remains of those abbeys which first brought the area under cultivation in the twelfth and thirteenth centuries. Paul Wagret writes of even the greatest of these abbeys, so few miles from the river that in the minds of many visitors it is on the Loire: 'The former wilderness-frontier of Fontevrault retains, eight centuries after Robert d'Arbrissel (its founder) many a wood and heath on its sandy soil.'

These regions formed natural frontiers. What remains of the ancient forest of Gâtine still divides Touraine (Indre-et-Loire) from the Bas-Vendômois (now part of Loir-et-Cher), just as earlier it divided the Turones from the Carnutes (the two Gallic tribes who have given their names to Tours and Chartres).

On the edge of the *gâtine*, where it drops to the Val, lie the best of the Loire vineyards. This is indicated by the name *coteau*, meaning hillside or slope, which many of them have. The vine thrives not on a rich soil, but on exposure to the sun, which as far north as this can only be guaranteed by a southward slope protected from the wind.

Although Bourgueil, Chinon, Saché, and the Coteaux du Layon are not strictly speaking part of the Val, they make a vital contribution to the culture of the Loire Valley. This is not just because they are wine-producing areas. A civilisation springing from the alluvial Val alone would be too luxuriant to qualify for that term of praise *le juste milieu*. In both geographical and human terms the austere *gâtine* redresses 'the so valued balance of the Tourangeau character – Rabelais corrected by Descartes'.

4

Bocage

Bocage is a puzzling word to an Englishman. It is used by the French as if it refers to some unusual phenomenon, and sometimes suggests that there is something mysterious about the people who live there.

Yet the average visitor from across the Channel may well feel, after crossing the depressing sugar-beet fields of Picardy, the interminable corn plateau of the Beauce, or even the confusing blend of the Val and *gâtine* which constitutes Touraine, that in entering *pays bocager* he is coming home.

Bocage is simply hedgeland: little fields and meadows divided by hedges. At first sight it has a similarity with Britain almost everywhere south of the Highlands.

But after looking a little more closely, you will notice how small the fields are: few reach five acres and their average size is only one or two. The landowners who planted most of the English hedges when they 'enclosed' their land in the eighteenth and early nineteenth centuries insisted on much larger, economically more viable fields, so that their tenant farmers would be prosperous, and could afford to pay good rents.

The divisions between these little fields do not consist merely of vegetation – bushes and brambles and the occasional tree – but of vegetation growing on top of, and from the sides of, banks of earth. They would take more effort to remove than the hedges of Midland and Southern England.

The reason is that they are much older than most of their English counterparts. Look at a hunting print showing the Quorn streaming across the uplands near Melton Mowbray in about 1830. They have as many jumps to make as they would riding across the same countryside today, but the obstacles which face them are merely fences. Often, however, there is a suggestion of growth at the base of these fences. This is the infancy of the hedgerows of modern Leicestershire.

The hedges of the French *bocage*, on the other hand, were at that date every bit as dense and as continuous as they are now. Forty years earlier they had provided cover for the royalist rebels who rocked the Revolutionary government in Paris.

North of the Loire these rebels were known as the *chouans*, from Jean Chouan, one of their leaders (and not, as is often said, from the owl-hoot they used as a signal – *chouette* means 'screech-owl'). To the south they were called the *vendéens*, from the department which was their heartland. Both might better have been named the *bocagers*. For the *bocage* provided the terrain adapted to their guerilla tactics of ambush and hit-and-run raid. It also provided their recruiting ground.

In conferring these advantages on the rebels, it at the same time restricted their action. For once in open country, they were no match for the regular armies of the Republic. Away from their own dense hedgeland they were deprived, too, of their best asset, the support of the population among whom they were operating. They could only advance as far as Le Mans before their crushing defeat. Only once did *chouans* and *vendéens* manage to link across the narrow strip which divided them, the Loire Valley itself.

The history of the royalist rebels goes some way towards explaining the mystery of the *bocage* for other Frenchmen. It is still hard to penetrate, once they leave the straight roads with which Napoleon criss-crossed it to bring it under control. The inhabitants, even today, differ in many of their basic attitudes from those of the more open regions to the east.

The *bocage* is essentially a phenomenon of the West, in the sense in which the word is used inside France. In this sense the Basque country is not in the West, nor is Bordeaux, nor even perhaps La Rochelle. These all belong to the South-West, which is in turn an outlying part of the Midi, the South. The true West is everything north of the Marais *poitevin* and west of the Paris basin (the country drained by the Seine and its tributaries). The area is outlined by the

Région Ouest of French Railways, with its Paris terminus at the Gare Montparnasse. It consists of western Normandy, western Maine, western Anjou, western Poitou (the Vendée), and the whole of Brittany. It corresponds broadly with the Armorican massif, with its historical Celtic background.

Bocage seems to be the landscape in regions where Celtic influence was deepest and longest-lasting. For this reason, it might be more easily understood by a Welshman than an Englishman.

Certain Englishmen, however, will at once recognise in these tiny fields with hedge-topped banks, and in these deep, leafy lanes, the landscape of their own county. It is the county which formed the far western and most Celtic corner of Wessex – Devon.

Downstream from Angers, the Loire Valley, instead of laying a fertile strip amid the *gâtines*, cuts a narrow corridor between two regions of muddy *bocage*. The southern one, the Mauges, is described by Paul Wagret as 'a profoundly rural region, a wild region which served as the centre of the insurrection of 1793. Its appearance above the pleasing Valley is as disturbing as a barrier. Kléber (a republican general who fought the vendéens) called it "the labyrinth" . . . The strategic roads of the nineteenth century (built, as mentioned earlier, to keep it under control), contemptuous of the villages, run dead straight across silent countryside.'

The Segréen, the *bocage* immediately to the north of the Loire, has a more obvious name, from the pleasant market town of Segré, clustered beside the Oudon, a little tributary of the Mayenne. (Most of the *pays*, the natural economic regions, to the north of the Loire, are equally unimaginatively named: Baugeois from Baugé, Vendô-mois from Vendôme, Pays manceau from Le Mans, Dunois from Châteaudun). But the Segréen is just as grim as the Mauges when contrasted with the Valley, perhaps even more so, since slates here replace tiles on roofs. This is why it is sometimes known as 'l'Anjou noir'. There is a black stain even on its social relations, for the Segréen is the only district in France north of the Loire where the tenants customarily hold their land by *métayage*, an archaic relic of serfdom based on crop-sharing.

This survival of *métayage* may be one reason why countrymen from districts to the north, just as *bocager* in landscape, but with a firm tradition of freeholding, have told me that they feel profoundly ill at ease as they come south towards the pig-producing centre of Craon, or the goose-fattening town of Château-Gontier.

Yet their own countryside is no less mysterious to the outsider.
The *bocage* everywhere, viewed by another writer, P. George, from
one of its low hills, 'in the distant bluish haze, seems an immense
forest. Not everything is illusion in this vision. The *bocage* emanates
from the forest, it gradually separates itself from it . . . it has grown
from it over the course of the centuries.'

This slow development from primeval woodland is the essential
difference between the hedgeland of western France and that of
most of England. It does not always mean that much of the original
forest survives. Like 'leafy Warwickshire', it has plenty of individual
trees, but few concentrations of them. It is in the more northerly
parts of the *bocage*, those of the freeholding tradition, that there are
blocks of forest comparable to those of the *gâtines* and of the country
between the *rivières*. There they crown the highest points of our
region, small hills which seem like mountains after the gentle valleys,
the low *gâtine* plateaux, and the still lower Sologne. The name
'Alpes Mancelles' is given to one such miniature range, and 'Corniche
du Pail' to the road crossing another.

Their wooded summits add to their seeming height, and give a
sombre, mysterious background to the many interesting places in
scarcely visited north-west Maine. None is more sombre nor more
mysterious than the Mont des Avaloirs, above the *bocage* to the
south. It deserves the respect it demands, for it not only forms the
frontier between Maine and Normandy, but its height, 1,390 feet,
makes it the highest point west of the Morvan in Burgundy, or
north of the Massif Central. It marks the watershed where streams,
instead of running north to empty their waters in the Channel, join
tributary after tributary until eventually they flow into the Loire.

The

HISTORICAL BACKGROUND

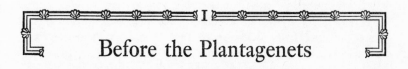

I

Before the Plantagenets

The Loire Valley had a central place in European history under the Plantagenets, and again, later, under the Valois. But its role in prehistoric times was perhaps even more significant. It supplied the best of the stone required by the techniques of the Old Stone Age (before 20,000 B.C.) and of the New Stone Age (20,000 to 2000 B.C.).

This stone was the flint of Le Grand Pressigny, a village thirty miles south of Tours, on a tributary of a tributary of the Loire, now with a Renaissance château standing within mediaeval ramparts. The château has become a museum where characteristic flints are on display.

The advantage of Pressigny flint was that it was found as 'pounds of butter' – of the shape and colour of the old-fashioned farmhouse variety – which were easily split up. The 'blades' into which it shattered were exported all over Europe and North Africa, sometimes already carved and polished into implements or weapons, but often in unfinished form for making up as required on arrival.

Such a long-distance trade required communications. Even without help from archaeology, it is clear that Tours already marked an important crossing of the Loire, and that the route south-east along the Cher, avoiding the marshy Sologne, was already in regular use.

With the introduction of metals, the population increased thanks to more advanced farming techniques and tended to concentrate in places which have remained inhabited centres ever since.

The metal which revolutionised prehistoric life was iron, and the people who brought it to France were the Celts. It enabled them to establish themselves as the ruling élite of the tribes which faced Caesar during his conquest of Gaul. These tribes were each independent, but shared certain traditions and beliefs. Their sense of a common nationality was expressed most dramatically when their elders and Druids met each year at St-Benoît, between Orléans and Gien. The Loire at this period was as important historically as it has ever been.

Many of the Gallic villages can still be recognised by their names. Thus Bourgueil, famous for its fine red wine, and the many villages called Montreuil, owe their -*euil* suffix to what was originally the Gallic *ialos*, signifying a clearing in the primeval forest. Bléré, where the road from Amboise to Loches crosses the Cher, is a derivation of the Gallic *briva*, marking a bridge. Braye, Brée and Brèches are modified versions of the Gallic *briga* implying height, although this is often only because they dominate some steep little valley beneath them.

Ingrandes, twenty miles downstream from Angers, stands at the frontier not only of the modern *départements* of Maine-et-Loire and Loire-Atlantique, but of the ancient provinces of Anjou and Brittany. But there are four other Ingrandes in the region, all called after the Gallic word *icoranda*.

Ingrandes-de-Touraine, now ten miles inside Indre-et-Loire, marks the pre-1790 frontier between Touraine and Anjou, but also the pre-56 B.C. frontier between Turones and Andecaves. The others marked the frontiers between these Turones* (whose capital is now called Tours) and the Carnutes (with capital Chartres), the Pictones (with capital Poitiers), and the Bituriges (with capital Bourges).

These, together with Le Mans and Orléans (Roman name Aurelianis), and smaller places like Vendôme (Vindocinum) and Châteaudun (Castrodunum) were taken over and developed as urban centres after the Roman conquest. Even today, the roads between them have for long stretches that tell-tale straightness associated with Watling Street or the Fosse Way. For three hundred years the commerce of a peaceful but lightly-populated empire passed along them unmolested, beneath the still surviving brick tower at Cinq-Mars, the aqueduct behind Luynes which supplied Tours with water, or the post-house at Thézée beside the Cher.

Without problems of space or security, the towns grew as garden cities, spreading far beyond the minimum living area required for their population. The invasions and civil war of the mid-third

---

* The Turones also gave their name to the distant German province of Thuringia.

century caused a sudden contraction. Tours in early Roman times covered more than two hundred and fifty acres. After A.D. 275 it was packed behind ramparts which sealed off less than ten acres between the cathedral and the Loire.

You can get an idea of what these late Roman towns looked like from Jublains, near Mayenne, up in the far north-west of the region. There a small town, originally spread over an area larger than the present village, was replaced by a fortress-settlement, whose grim outer walls, fifteen feet high and as many thick, surround a rectangle of a mere three and a half acres. It was captured and deserted about A.D. 275, so its ruins have remained largely intact.

The other Roman cities of the region lived on in their reduced circumstances. They even acquired a new importance as the sees of the Christian bishops, who began to take on some of the responsibilities of government as imperial authority declined.

Christianity had arrived late, a century later than in southern Gaul, and two centuries later than in Rome. But it was lucky in the quality of its converts, in particular of Martin, a soldier born in what is now Yugoslavia, who was elected Bishop of Tours in 371.

The well known story of how he split his cloak in two to share it with a beggar illustrates his down-to-earth religion. The practical good sense of this literally warming gesture appealed to the inhabitants of a northern, Atlantic region far more than the sophisticated arguments of Arius and Athanasius, which divided their contemporaries beside the Mediterranean, could have done.

None of these cities was ever an intellectual centre of the standing of Bordeaux. The Roman theatre at Tours is more likely to have been used for light entertainment – mimes and jugglers – than the plays of Plautus and Terence. Nor was St Martin an intellectual. But his combination of saintly character and administrative ability left two permanent legacies.

Until his time Christianity in northern Gaul had been confined to the towns. Even as late as the ninth century a book of services (now in the municipal library of Le Mans) contains a prayer against idols and pagan temples. It was he who began the conversion of the countryfolk (in Latin the *pagani*). The number of parish churches in the region which are dedicated to St Martin witness the respect and affection with which he was regarded. It was this that brought pilgrims to his tomb outside the walls of Tours, and hence prestige and authority to the city and its bishop. It was in places of such

religious and commercial importance that learning survived in the
Dark Ages. As a result, Tours now acquired a cultural significance
it had never had under Rome.

Two centuries after St Martin, Bishop Gregory of Tours wrote in
rough and ready Latin a *History of the Franks*, without which our
knowledge of the violent world of the early Merovingian kings would
be even more fragmentary than it is. A further two centuries later,
the English scholar Alcuin, Abbot of St Martin of Tours, founded
there a school of philosophy and theology which was one of the
principal centres of the brief cultural revival sometimes called the
Carolingian Renaissance.

The Loire, which had been near the edge of the Roman Empire,
was at the heart of the revived Empire of Charlemagne. A hundred
miles upstream from Tours, where the Druids had met every year
long before the conquest of Caesar, the abbey of Fleury was founded
in the middle of the seventh century. The choice of this ancient holy
place was probably deliberate. In 673 a party of monks brought back
the body of St Benedict from Monte Cassino in southern Italy, and
thus gave Fleury both Christian associations and the chief place in
the Benedictine order which the saint had founded.

Learning was part of the Benedictine way of life. The school of
Fleury had five thousand pupils in the time of Charlemagne, and
these and its monks transcribing and illuminating manuscripts,
made it amount to a ninth-century university.

During the Dark Ages the Loire twice acted briefly as a frontier
between North and South. From 475 to 507 it separated the powerful Visigoths from the Romans who still held northern Gaul, and
then from the Franks who finally conquered it in 486. This period
ended with the defeat of the Visigoths by the Frankish king Clovis
at Vouillé near Poitiers in 507.

In 732 the Arabs, who had only twenty years earlier crossed the
Straits of Gibraltar, brought an army right up to the Loire Valley.
The decisive victory of the Franks under Charles Martel, the real
founder of the Carolingian dynasty, took place on the Landes du
Ruchard, a vast clearing in the Forest of Chinon, on the 'peninsula'
formed by the Indre, Vienne and Loire. The Moslem prisoners, it
is said, were interned and settled on the Véron, the tip of this
peninsula. Levéel himself considers that the people there are still
noticeably darker than their neighbours.

At other times, the region was ruled as a unity for over nine hundred years, from the conquest by Caesar to the grandsons of Charlemagne. Sometimes this rule was weak. The capital moved from place to place as the Frankish kings or the later Carolingian emperors divided or reunited their realm. Once or twice it was at Orléans, at others at Tours, Angers or Le Mans, but all formed part of the same political entity.

This unity, and the revived learning of Tours and Fleury, were shattered by the Viking attacks which ravaged Western Europe from the second half of the ninth century. Although the Loire is a poor waterway for regular commercial traffic, to seamen who had taken their ships to Iceland, or up tiny English streams, it was an open highway to the heart of the continent.

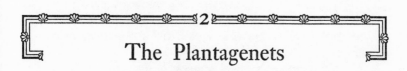

The Plantagenets

From 850 to 950 was the darkest century of the Dark Ages, in the Loire Valley as elsewhere in Europe. The 'Francia' which emerged from it was a lesser thing than the Frankish Empire of Charlemagne. Where the Vikings had been halted or defeated, this had been achieved not by the imperial government, but by local leaders with locally raised forces. Although many of these leaders had the title *comes* (count), which Charlemagne had given only to his personal representatives, they and their descendants ruled completely independent areas.

The old Roman cities of Angers, Le Mans and Tours each became the centre of a county, as did the smaller Roman towns of Châteaudun and Vendôme. So also did two strategically situated fortresses which now became important for the first time: Laval, on a hill with two summits beside the Mayenne; and Blois, on a rocky promontory above the Loire, halfway between Tours and Orléans. The political history of the tenth and eleventh centuries in the Loire Valley is largely that of the rivalry of these counties, and in particular of Blois with Anjou.

The ruling families of both possessed remarkable energy and

vitality. Their Counts found expression not only in fighting each other and invading their neighbours, but in building. In this region you will often find that a church was founded by Thibault le Tricheur ('the Cheat') of Blois, or that a château stands on a site originally fortified by Foulques Nerra ('the Black') of Anjou.

These two outsize personalities had other interests. Thibault I le Tricheur (died 978) built the first castle at Saumur, as well as rebuilding its monastery. And the fierce Foulques III Nerra (972–1040) took time off from fighting to make three pilgrimages to Jerusalem. Their successors, too, often found it hard to distinguish the claims of their counties from those of their Church.

The close association of the religious and the secular in the Middle Ages was closest of all in these earliest centuries. Not only learning, but the most basic records and administration – everything which would today be carried out by a Civil Service – depended upon the Church. It even led the way in the greatest achievement of these centuries, hardly mentioned in history books, but infinitely more important for the future of the region than the petty exploits of the Counts of Blois or Vendôme, Anjou or Laval.

This achievement was the 'conquest of the soil' which, by clearing new land and bringing it under cultivation, quadrupled the population of France. The process was uneven. Certain areas, such as Provence, had already been settled in Roman times, and were still suffering from the disturbances to traffic in the Mediterranean. To bring about the over-all increase in prosperity which occurred between the ninth and the fourteenth centuries other regions must have developed all the more.

This is certainly true here, particularly in Anjou and Maine. For example, although the *bocage*, with its small fields divided by banks and hedges, is characteristic of lands where Celtic influence has been strongest, the north and west of Maine – countryside as typically *bocager* as any – contains hardly a Celtic place-name. The reason is that before the eleventh century this whole area was uninhabited forest. Church records show that Maine contained fewer than two hundred parishes in the ninth century, immediately before the Viking raids, but more than six hundred in the fourteenth, immediately before the Hundred Years War.

Even where settlement did exist, it was thin on the ground. A gift made in 572 to the abbey of St-Vincent shows that the villa of Tresson, which has given its name to a village to the south of the main road from Le Mans to Orléans, stretched from north to south over ten miles, covering ten modern *communes*. Yet most of this tract of some twenty-five square miles must have remained unused, for the total work-force consisted of only ten serfs, one of whom was permanently employed in caring for a herd of horses.

Even the Loire Valley itself was still not completely cleared for cultivation, especially downstream at its junction with the Authion and the Maine. This 'valley of Anjou' was covered by the forgotten forests of Beaufort-la-Vallée and of Bellepoule, reaching all the way to Angers.

The *seigneurs* throughout the region did well from the revolution which during the eleventh, twelfth and thirteenth centuries felled the forests, ploughed up the heaths (*landes*), and rooted out the spinneys (*épinaies*). The villages which rose in their place, with names like St Hilaire-des-Landes, Landerande, Bois-Robert and L'Epinay, gave them more subjects and bigger revenues.

It was the Counts of Anjou and of Maine who did best of all, for their lands started from a lower level of development. They had greater stretches of woodland and heath available for colonisation by conversion, in the local tradition, into *bocage*.

The long succession of Angevin Counts, Foulques I 'the Red', Foulques II 'the Good', Geoffroi I 'Greyfish', the castle-builder Foulques III Nerra 'the Black', Geoffroi II 'the Hammer', Geoffroi III 'the Bearded', Foulques IV 'the Surly', Geoffroi IV, another 'Hammer', and Foulques V 'the Young', each defended and added to a little state which was steadily growing not only externally by conquest, but internally by the agricultural skill of their subjects.

These Counts of Anjou had an advantage over their rivals in not sharing a common frontier with the two most dangerous of all the feudal states in France. The first of these was that of the Normans, Vikings who instead of returning home settled round Rouen, rapidly absorbed Christian culture, and went on to improve on it. The greatest Duke of Normandy, William, conquered Maine before he conquered England. His expedition across the Channel gave the *manceaux* the opportunity to rise against him.

The second dangerous neighbour for Blois and Maine was less of a military menace – at least for the two centuries after 987. But it made up for its apparent weakness in two ways, first in prestige: its rulers were none other than the Kings of France. This 'France' was merely the westernmost of the three divisions into which the grandsons of Charlemagne split up the Empire of 'Francia'. When the last Carolingians were replaced in 987 by the election of their greatest vassal, Hugh Capet, 'France' shrank still further, and the term was often used to describe only the territories that he and his successors directly controlled. This is how the phrase 'Île de France' has come to be used for the district immediately round Paris.

Their personal rule hardly extended beyond these narrow limits. Yet they remained Kings, with certain theoretical rights over all the Dukes and Counts and other lords further down the feudal hierarchy, and with all the grandeur of the inheritors of Charlemagne and Clovis.

Their weakness was compensated for in another, more practical way. The 'royal domain' might be small, but it was central, and contained the variety and fertility of the soils to feed the growing city of Paris. It also controlled the middle courses of two great rivers: the territory of the early Capetians, tiny though it was, straddled both the Seine and the Loire. The section they owned was the extremity of its great northern bend, where long ago it had once turned north to become a tributary of the Seine. It was also the section where the upstream traffic from Nantes met the downstream traffic from the Massif Central at the old Roman city of Orléans. For over a century this was the royal residence as often as was Paris.

In the eleventh century, the Loire came as near as it ever did to becoming the capital of France. The ring of great Gothic cathedrals, Chartres, Beauvais, Soissons and Sens, which later rose around Paris, and under Parisian inspiration, had not yet been built; but Orléans already had the vast Romanesque abbey of St-Benoît at Fleury, with its prestige inherited from Charlemagne and the Gauls before him.

The poor kings needed all this royal prestige to withstand their powerful vassals, especially after the Counts of Blois became also Counts of Champagne, and after the Dukes of Normandy in 1066 became Kings of England. They tried to play on the balance of power, helping Anjou to capture Touraine from Blois, and assisting both against Normandy.

Later, however, they were helped by the quarrels between William the Conqueror's sons. And when the youngest of these sons, Henry I, died in 1135, the families of Normandy and Blois became embroiled in a war for the throne of England. The Blois contender, Stephen, an active knight whom the feudal lords of England preferred to Henry I's daughter Matilda, claimed his title through his mother, a sister of Henry I who had married a Count of Blois. For a few years Louis VI and Louis VII were able to relax in Paris, knowing that their neighbours were fully occupied.

Their satisfaction was increased by the marriage of Louis VII in 1137 to the heiress of the last Count of Poitou. She was also Duchess of Aquitaine, and thus brought her husband the overlordship of the whole South-West, from the Pyrenees almost up to the Loire. Blois and Anjou were dwarfed by this vast addition of territory.

It was personal factors which halted the expansion of the French monarchy. The first such factor was the vigour of the ruling family of Anjou. The fifth Foulques, 'the Young', after ruling successfully for a quarter of a century, went off on a Crusade in 1129. In Palestine he married Melisande, the daughter of the King of Jerusalem. In due course he succeeded his father-in-law, and spent the last twelve years of his life ruling that kingdom.

His County he left behind him to his sixteen-year-old son, the fifth Geoffroi, whom he had married in 1128 to Matilda of England. She was eleven years older than him, and already the widow of the Emperor of Germany.

Geoffroi, called by the English Geoffrey, was known as 'le bel Plantagenêt' from the sprig of broom (*plante de genêt*) he carried on his helmet. On his father-in-law's death he succeeded in occupying Maine and Normandy. He devoted his life to strengthening this compact group of possessions north of the Loire, and it was his wife who led the abortive invasion of England in 1141.

He was buried in the cathedral of Le Mans, the central city of his dominions. Its museum displays his portrait in a coloured enamel which once decorated his tomb.

After his death, personal factors continued to favour the Plantagenets, as the Angevin rulers were now known. For a start, there was a quarrel between Louis VII and Eleanor of Aquitaine, which came to a head during their return together from the Second Crusade. The story of his well-founded suspicions of her infidelity, of their temporary reconciliation by the Pope, who elaborately decorated a double bed in his efforts to end their estrangement, and of her bitter complaints that her husband had the morals of a monk, reads like an article in today's popular Sunday Press.

Just before he died, Geoffrey Plantagenet came to Paris to

negotiate a treaty, accompanied by his son Henry. The interest shown in this eighteen-year-old by Eleanor, although she was twenty-nine, added Louis's jealousy to the royal couple's mutual incompatibility. With an unthinking personal spite amounting to madness, the King dragged her round Aquitaine, pulling down his fortresses and withdrawing his garrisons. Then he summoned an ecclesiastical council at Beaugency on the Loire to declare the marriage dissolved, on the grounds that its partners were too closely related.

Eleanor travelled by night back to her own lands, giving the slip to her many suitors, who desired her possessions as much as her person. The suitor she did meet, Henry, desired both. She married him less than two months later, in May 1152.

Some men seek a wife who reminds them of their mother. The difference in age between Eleanor and Henry was the same as that between Matilda and Geoffrey. Both women had difficult personalities, and both were also heiresses; and Henry was not prepared to surrender any portion of either of their inheritances. In 1153 he landed in England, and forced Stephen of Blois to accept him as heir to the kingdom which had been his grandfather's.

On Stephen's death the following year, the area which history books sometimes call the 'Angevin Empire' stretched from the Scottish border to the Pyrenees. At its largest, a few years later, its dependencies included Scotland, Ireland, and Brittany.

'Empire' is a misleading word to describe this assorted collection of feudal fiefs, each held on different terms, and united only in the person of their ruler. But the fact that this was their only link makes the term 'Angevin' most appropriate. To Henry II, born at Le Mans, and heir to the long line of Foulques and Geoffrois, Anjou and Maine were not only the centre of his realm, but his homeland. In his decline, he retired into that homeland when family and fortune turned against him.

He was brought low not by his quarrel with Thomas à Becket, nor by the accession in 1180 of a new young king in Paris, but by his differences with his sons. They were influenced against him by their mother, as the tempestuous love of the couple turned to bitter hatred. Created by personal links, the Angevin Empire foundered on personal animosity. After accepting a humiliating treaty forced on him in 1189 at Chinon, by Philip II of France in alliance with his son Richard, Henry died two days later after hearing that his youngest and favourite son, John, had also turned against him. He was only fifty-six. Although these last scenes of his life were scarcely imperial, their setting at Chinon was in the Plantagenet heartland.

It was at Chinon, too, according to an ancient tradition, that his son Richard Coeur-de-Lion was carried to die ten years later, when his career, which carried the Angevin name to the shores of the Mediterranean, was ended ignominiously by a stray arrow at a remote castle on the edge of the Massif Central.

The Plantagenet power at this moment might seem as solid as it had ever been. Richard's successor, John, by his first marriage to the daughter of a Count of Savoy, had even brought Italy within the Angevin horizon. But personally linked empires depend on personalities. John had all the headstrong impulsiveness of his family, but lacked either his father's capacity for hard work, or his brother's qualities of leadership. His opponent was perhaps the shrewdest king France ever had.

Philip II's trump card was his position as ultimate feudal overlord, to whom in the last resort the Plantagenet vassals could appeal over the Angevin's head. He played it to devastating effect when certain lords of Aquitaine, together with John's nephew Arthur, were captured by the English King in 1202. This gave Philip the excuse to pronounce a sentence of disinheritance and confiscation.

He carried it into effect by steadily conquering Normandy over the next two years, and then going on to occupy Maine, Touraine and Anjou in 1205. Royal seneschals and bailiffs moved down the Loire from Orléans, and the domain of the Capetians was pushed west all the way to the borders of Brittany. More than half a century passed before John's son Henry III accepted this *fait accompli* at the Treaty of Paris in 1259. After this the Plantagenets were no longer Angevin.

But one corner of Anjou remained, and still remains, Plantagenet. In the great Romanesque abbey church of Fontevrault, three miles south of where the Vienne meets the Loire, three larger-than-life statues carved from the local tufa mark the graves of Henry II, Eleanor, and their son Richard. A smaller wooden figure is that of Isabelle d'Angoulême, widow of John and mother of Henry III, who was buried here too, although she died more than forty years after the Valois conquest.

British governments have often sought to transfer these tombs to Westminster or Windsor. During the personal friendship of Queen

Victoria with the Empress Eugénie, this was about to be achieved, but the Franco-Prussian war intervened, and the three continue to lie in their native soil.

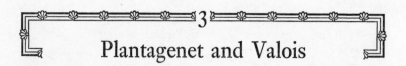

3

Plantagenet and Valois

After 1205 in practice, and after 1259 by treaty, the Plantagenets no longer ruled in their native Loire Valley. But they continued to exercise some control over the more distant parts of Eleanor's Aquitaine. Although they now drew their power from England, their court remained almost as French as in the days when it was more frequently at Chinon or Tours than at Winchester or Westminster. They were still French-speaking, French-thinking, and often French-marrying princes.

This tendency to cement peace treaties, or to conclude successful negotiations, with a marriage alliance led to the second long conflict between the Plantagenets and the French monarchy. Their opponents were now no longer the elder branch of the Capetians they had fought during the so-called 'First Hundred Years War' between 1159 and 1259.

After Philip II that branch had gone on to produce the brilliant rulers St Louis and Philip the Fair. But early in the fourteenth century it burnt itself out in a succession of squalid kings well named by Maurice Druon in his cycle of historical novels, now made into a television series: *Les rois maudits*.

The death of the last of these 'accursed kings' in 1328 left France for the first time in 340 years without a king's son to succeed to the throne. The story of how Edward III of England claimed this through his mother, a daughter of Philip the Fair, and of how his claim was invalidated by the 'Salic Law' is part of general European history. So is the second and better known Hundred Years War which followed.

There is also a more particular local interest. The nearest claimant through the male line required by the Salic Law was Philippe de

Valois, who as Philip VI introduced the dynasty which so influenced the Loire Valley. In a sense this dynasty was just as Angevin as its enemies, for Philippe de Valois was the heir to the County of Anjou, re-created by St Louis for one of his brothers.

The fortunes of the War sometimes brought the Plantagenet armies back to their family lands. These periods were only brief. The English campaigns generally concentrated on the accessible northern provinces (where the battles of Crécy and Agincourt were fought), or on the South-West where the Plantagenets were still Dukes of Gascony and Guienne. But every now and again a *chevauchée* – a mixture of knightly pageantry and ruthless raid – would stream across France from one place to another, crossing the Loire in the process – for example, that of the Black Prince in 1356, led to the English victory at Poitiers.

It was only at a late stage in the war that the Loire became the main battlefield. This happened when the government of the infant Henry VI, established by his father's victories as King in both London and Paris, determined to drive the uncrowned French Dauphin from the remains of his inheritance, consisting of the Loire Valley and certain adjoining provinces. 'Le roi de Bourges', as he was nicknamed, divided his time between that city and his fortress on the Loire. The first step in dislodging him was to be the capture of Orléans, the Capetians' own original base on the river, from which two and a quarter centuries earlier they had themselves been driven downstream.

The arrival of the besieging English armies in October 1428 brought the fight to the Loire in earnest. The visitor will get an incoherent picture of the events of 1429 from the memorials to them that he will find up and down the Valley. So here is a brief summary of them in chronological order.

The English forces were too few to 'dig in' right round the city, which was therefore still more or less in touch with the outside world. This gave importance to the various fortified posts on the outskirts, from which the besiegers tried to complete their blockade, and the capture of which was to be vital to the relief.

It was Jeanne d'Arc, the Maid of Orléans, who was to lift the siege. She first reached the Loire at Gien on 1st March, having come all the way from Lorraine. Her small party crossed the Sologne and went through Loches to reach Chinon a week later. Her famous recognition of the Dauphin masquerading as a courtier, when she entered the hall of the château of Chinon, took place on March 9th.

Having convinced him of her mission, she set off at the head of the relieving army via Tours and Blois, approaching Orléans by the left bank. She was surprised to learn that it lay on the other side of the river, but crossed this on April 28th, and managed to enter the city the next day with one of the food convoys.

As so often in her brief career, she showed a shrewd psychological grasp in thus identifying herself with the besieged. Her first active steps, the capture of the Bastille St-Loup on May 4th, of the convent of the Augustins on May 6th, and of the Tourelles fort commanding the southern end of the bridge across the Loire on May 7th, were as much a break-out by them as a relief by outside forces.

Next day the English raised the siege. Jeanne d'Arc, though wounded in the breast at the Tourelles, was able to take the field. On June 12th, twelve miles further west at Jargeau, she defeated an English army beside the Loire. Six days later, fifteen miles to the north-west of Orléans in the open Beauce, she again beat them in a pitched battle at Patay.

It was along the Loire, royal as never before, that she led her Dauphin from Chinon to Gien on the way to his coronation at Reims on July 17th. And it was near the river that the crowned Charles VII still preferred to live, even after the French victories which she had begun had caused the English to evacuate Paris in 1437.

Although Jeanne herself was captured in 1430, and burned at Rouen in 1431, the French armies continued to press their advantage. They were often led by her friend Dunois, puzzlingly nicknamed 'the bastard of Orléans'. The 'bastard' came from his being the illegitimate son of the Duke of Orléans, whose assassination by the Burgundians in 1407 sharpened the resistance of the Orléanais in 1429. The Dunois is the region around Châteaudun on the upper Loir thirty miles north-west of Orléans, of which he was made Count.

When Dunois had reconquered Normandy, and finally occupied Bordeaux and Bayonne, which had been Plantagenet possessions ever since 1152, the defeated English armies went home to tear each other to pieces in the Wars of the Roses. Not only the old aristocratic families of England perished in that conflict. As a later Chief Justice of England could ask:

'Where is Bohun? Where's Mowbray? Where's Mortimer? . . .
Nay, which is more, and most of all, where is Plantagenet? They are
entombed in the urns and sepulchres of mortality.'

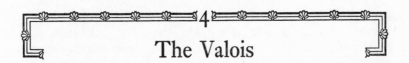

4

The Valois

The historian of Touraine, Pierre Levéel, has proudly and rightly
called the two great kings of the fifteenth century *les rois tour-
angeaux*.

Charles VII owed everything to the Loire Valley: his wife, Marie
d'Anjou, to whom he was married when they were both children;
his base when the rest of his kingdom was occupied by the enemy;
the victory at Orléans which marked the turn of the tide of his fortunes; and his dearly loved mistress, Agnès Sorel, whose superb
breast, thinly disguised as that of the Virgin, forever suckles in Jean
Fouquet's intimate and pleasing portrait.

His favourite residences, Chinon and Loches, where he estab-
lished a court as sumptuous as that of his rivals the Dukes of
Burgundy, were in Touraine. So was that of his son, Louis XI, at
Plessis-lès-Tours, just outside the capital.

But there flourished in the Valley during these years two other,
artistically more brilliant courts: Anjou and Orléans. They occupy
little space in political histories because their princes were closely
related to the King and on good terms with him.

The connection of the Valois with Anjou came not only from the
child-marriage of Charles VII, but from the fact that the dynasty's
founder, Philippe de Valois, had been Count of Anjou before he
became King of France. In the early fifteenth century the House of
Anjou, descended from the second son of the French King who had
been captured at Poitiers, was not only the most powerful in the
West of France, but also ruled Provence, and claimed a string of
shadowy titles ranging from King of the two Sicilies to King of
Jerusalem. Such insubstantial claims can be a handicap: an earlier
Count of Anjou had lost an army and a kingdom in the Sicilian

Vespers. His descendant, the well-loved 'roi René' presided at Angers over a fairytale court appropriate to the unreal world of his dreams.

Almost as soon as René was dead, in 1481, his hard-headed cousin, Louis XI, showed both a typical acquisitiveness and his love of the Loire in adding Anjou to the French royal domain.

The other court was that of the Dukes of Orléans. The first of these, uncle of Charles VII and father of the illegitimate Dunois, was the royal prince assassinated in 1407. His widow shut herself in a room draped in black at the château of Blois, where she died after a year 'of anger and mourning'.

It was at Blois, too, that their son Charles, who had earlier been captured at Agincourt, set up the gayest of the three fifteenth-century Loire palaces in 1441. As the head of a cadet branch of the Valois he had no dynastic ambitions. Twenty-five years of permissive captivity in England had trained him as a poet rather than as an intriguer. Once free, he became a Renaissance Prince devoid of Machiavellian statecraft. That he left to his second cousin at Plessis-lès-Tours, just as he left regrets for the mediaeval past to that charming anachronism Le roi René.

These two cultured courts of Angers and of Blois were in friendly contact. Charles d'Orléans often received in his relaxed *nonchaloir* René d'Anjou, Jean de Bourbon, and other *seigneurs* of literary tastes passing through Blois. He would organise poetic debates for them and for other visiting poets and scholars. One of these, on the delightful theme 'I die of thirst beside the fountain', was won by an unknown twenty-six-year-old student from Paris, who had adopted as a name that of his protector's birthplace – Villon.

Part of François Villon's appeal lies in his appreciation of life at all levels. He certainly experienced this in the Loire Valley, from rubbing shoulders with such *neiges d'antan* as Le roi René at Blois, to imprisonment three years later at Orléans, and then at Meung-sur-Loire. That confinement at Orléans gives real force to that reference to

> *. . . Jehanne, la bonne Lorraine*
> *Qu'Englois brulerent a Rouan.*

It was at Meung that he wrote the *Grand Testament*, described by one critic as 'one of the most poignant cries of all literature'.

Charles d'Orléans was the least ambitious of the princes holding court in the Loire Valley in the mid-fifteenth century. Yet it was his own son who was to inherit the throne as Louis XII in 1498, on the accidental death without an heir of Charles VIII, the son of Louis XI.

Louis d'Orléans took over not only his predecessor's kingdom but his wife, Anne of Brittany, divorcing Louis XI's misshapen daughter Jeanne de France to do so. He did so out of genuine attraction for Anne, but also in order to ensure that her valuable Duchy was not lost to the crown.

This is yet another reminder of the importance of the Valley long before its 'great age'. Although the Loire estuary lies beyond the bounds of this guide, Nantes, its principal city and the capital of the two last and most powerful Dukes of Brittany, was until the marriage of Anne the seat of a fourth Loire court, combining much of the real power of Plessis-lès-Tours with something of the tradition of Angers and of the intellectual brilliance of Blois.

The golden age of the Loire coincided with the French Renaissance, though it is hard to give this an exact date. Charles d'Orléans and Louis XI had each in different ways certain of the qualities of Renaissance princes.

Many regard the campaign of Charles VIII in Italy as the beginning of the entry of Italian ideas and models into France. But he lost the rich loot of his baggage train at the battle of Fornovo in 1495, and remained a mediaeval figure until his death. Pierre Mesnard, founder of the *Centre d'Etudes Supérieures de la Renaissance* at Tours, considered that 'the death of Charles VIII marks the end of the French pre-Renaissance, which as yet owes nothing essential to Italy'. He believed it necessary to accept 'this capital fact of a French pre-Renaissance which placed the lands of the Loire in the adequate state of grace to provide welcome and naturalisation for the Italian Renaissance'.

This welcome was freely extended from the start of the sixteenth century. The influence of Italian masons and decorators, which had been subordinated to a mediaeval plan in Charles VIII's château of Amboise, first showed clearly at Blois under Louis XII and François I. And the sudden widening of the intellectual horizon, of which the new architecture was but an outward and visible sign, was even more dramatic.

It was also more specifically French. Writers transplant less easily than masons. Leonardo da Vinci spent the last three years of his life as the guest of François I at Le Clos Lucé, a stone's throw from where his compatriots were putting the finishing touches to the upper storey of the Louis XII wing at Amboise. But the voice of the French Renaissance had to be native.

It was perhaps more than coincidence that in the age when the Loire was the heart of France the voice should be that of a *tourangeau*. François Rabelais was born about 1440 at La Devinière, his family's modest country house five miles outside Chinon, where his father was an advocate. As a child he divided his time between the narrow streets of the little town, huddled between its castle hill and the Vienne, and the open countryside to the west.

That countryside, as literary critics often point out, provided him with the background for the activities of Gargantua and Pantagruel, the friendly giants who showed little respect for the old order which was breaking up in the second quarter of the sixteenth century.

However irreverent, Rabelais steered clear of the outright unorthodox. Such discretion was lacking in Clément Marot, who, although he was born at Cahors, spent much of his youth at Blois, where his father was secretary to Anne of Brittany.

His heresies were technical as well as doctrinal. In February 1526 he was imprisoned in the Châtelet at Paris after being denounced by his mistress for eating pork during Lent. He died in 1544 at Turin, where he fled after coming under suspicion of sympathising with the Reformers. But despite these Protestant leanings, and the similarity of his disordered life to that of Villon, whom he admired and edited, he celebrated in elegant verse the courts of François I and of his sister Marguerite d'Angoulême (whom he served for many years as *valet de chambre*).

Even more elegant, at home in royal courts, and liberated by the Renaissance, and even more rooted in this region were the next generation of poets, the famous Pléiade. Five of the seven had local origins: Joachim du Bellay from Liré on the Loire itself: Rémy Belleau from Nogent-le-Rotrou; Jean Antoine de Baïf from near La Flèche; J. Pelletier from Le Mans; and the greatest of them, Pierre de Ronsard, born in a manor beside the Loir.

Ronsard was the greatest French poet of the sixteenth century as Rabelais was the greatest prose writer. His life, if not his work, was even more closely associated with the region. Though his best known love poem was addressed to Hélène de Surgères, from Saintonge, he wrote it when already middle-aged. Those of his more passionate youth, such as *Mignonne, allons voir si la rose* were dedicated to Cassandre Salviati of Talcy, between Loir and Loire. He died on the bank of the Loire at St Cosme, a religious house a couple of miles downstream from Tours, of which he was lay prior during his last twenty years.

Ronsard lived simply at St Cosme; his diet can be easily followed today by shopping at the markets near his home.

> *L'artichot et la salade*
> *L'asperge et la pastenade*
> *Et les pépons tourangeaux*
> *Me sont herbes plus friandes*
> *Que les royales viandes*
> *Qui se servent par morceaux.*

But it was indulgence in those '*royales viandes*' in youth, without the compensating vegetable which made him, like all the wealthy of that time, an old man by the age of fifty.

Throughout his lifetime (1524–1585) '*royales viandes*' were being served beside the Loire. The biographer of François Premier, Desmond Seward, describes how 'during the first part of the reign, the royal wanderings tended to centre on the Loire Valley. His glittering court performed a Rabelaisian pilgrimage along the gentle river, from château to château, from forest to forest, picnicking beneath the trees at tables set for thousands.'

This Renaissance monarch *par excellence*, whose salamander crest is seen in many châteaux, moved to Fontainebleau and Paris after his return from captivity in Madrid, but his son and grandsons made extensive visits to their many homes in this region.

The two most important of these, Amboise and Blois, were the scenes of two grim episodes of the Wars of Religion which darkened the reigns of Henri II's three sons, another series of 'accursed kings' in whom the Valois dynasty ended.

Each of their reigns had its particularly horrific moment. The worst of all was the Massacre of St Bartholomew under Charles IX in 1572, centred on Paris. But the bloodiest moments of his brothers' reigns occurred beside the Loire.

The death of Henri II in 1559 meant that power would fall to whoever controlled his fifteen-year-old son, François II. When that control passed to the fiercely Catholic Guise family, the Protestants determined early in the following year to replace them by seizing the King.

Alerted, the Guises moved the court from Blois to Amboise. The conspirators switched their plans, and also made their way there, in small groups. But again their plans were betrayed, and their bands were picked off one by one. Their leader was killed in one such engagement in the *gâtine* north of the river.

There followed at the château a massacre which was largely responsible for the bitterness of the forty years of warfare which followed. The chief plotters were beheaded and the rank and file hanged from gallows, or directly from the battlements and the main balcony. There were rumours that Catherine de Médicis, with the young King and Queen (Mary Queen of Scots), had watched this as an after-dinner spectacle.

The power of the Guise family, and their popularity with the Catholics everywhere, with the enthusiastically Catholic Parisians in particular, only grew during the following thirty years. By 1588 the youngest of the three Valois brothers, Henri III, regarded them not as protectors but as enemies. He therefore summoned the States General in that year to Blois, where he hoped that the Guises would receive less support. But hostility to him rapidly increased among the gathering in the hall of the château, still called the Salle des États. Fearing that he might lose his crown, he decided on a pre-emptive strike.

Two days before Christmas, the Duke of Guise was summoned to the royal private apartments, where the perverted King's companion-bodyguards stabbed him to death. The second Guise brother, the Cardinal of Lorraine, was executed the following day.

Twelve days later, Catherine de Médicis died in her own suite in the château. The way was open for a reconciliation between the King, who had lost the support of the Catholics, and his cousin, the Protestant leader Henry of Navarre. Their combined armies laid siege to Paris.

One day late that summer of 1589 a young monk obtained a royal audience. A dagger that he had successfully concealed completed the trail of treachery begun at Amboise. The last Valois lay dead.

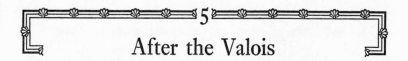

After the Valois

The extinction of the dynasty which had loved the Loire Valley very nearly coincided with the end of its golden age, and of its close connection with royalty. Henri IV was in the region at various times during the later stages of the Wars of Religion. And the Edict of Nantes which ended them was signed in 1598 in the city at the river's mouth.

But with the death in the following year of Gabrielle d'Estrées, his favourite from Touraine, he lost his incentive to accompany her on visits to her homeland. The Pays de la Loire entered the seventeenth century as provinces like any others.

Neither of its two greatest figures in this period spent much time there. Cardinal Richelieu was actually born in Paris, and probably never visited the grandiose palace he built beside the town which bears his name. This town as he reconstructed it, and the little that remains of his château, are a most inappropriate monument to the avowed enemy of feudal independence.

René Descartes was not only born at La Haye (now la Haye-Descartes) thirty miles south of Tours, but was also educated in the region, by the Jesuits of La Flèche. He spent his adult life elsewhere, mostly outside France. After some years as a soldier, he settled in Holland, a more congenial intellectual climate for a philosopher and mathematician.

In a more literal sense, the Dutch climate was less congenial, and right at the end of his life he exchanged it for a less congenial climate still. He had been invited to Sweden by that glamorous blue-stocking, Queen Christina. Homesickness made him hesitate to leave for 'this land of bears, between rocks and ice, a hesitation perfectly natural for one who was born in the gardens of Touraine'.

Like many other provinces in the eighteenth century, the region benefited from the skilful administration of good royal servants, in particular François-Pierre du Cluzel, Intendant of the Généralité of Tours from 1766 to 1783. He inaugurated the great stone bridge across the Loire which all visitors cross many times.

Like other regions, too, it had one or two progressive landowners. The Marquis of Turbilly, the chief spirit behind the *Société d'Agriculture d'Angers*, wrote a treatise on the bringing of wasteland under cultivation which became famous throughout Europe. The example he gave on his own property at Turbilly, near La Flèche, compared with that of his contemporaries 'Turnip' Townshend or Coke of Holkham across the Channel.

But unlike other provinces, the Loire Valley retained some share in the activities of the elegant and refined society of Paris and Versailles. The Duke of Sully entertained Voltaire. Rousseau spent a happy period as tutor to the Dupin family at Chenonceaux. Madame de Pompadour bought and transformed the château of Ménars.

Her favoured minister, the Duke of Choiseul, exiled from court after her death, retired to Chanteloup near Amboise. The friends he entertained there were a wittier and more fashionable society than that around his enemy Madame du Barry at Versailles. And although the gatherings around the Duke of Aiguillon at his château of Véretz near Tours were smaller, they were probably even more cultivated.

Nor was the life of the peasant as desperate here as in less fertile regions. When the Marquis of Argenson wrote that through lack of bread 'men are eating grass', he was using *l'herbe* as Ronsard did, to mean vegetables. Had they been as downtrodden as elsewhere, several of the major châteaux would have gone up in flames at the Revolution.

It was that explosion that brought to life the contrast between the Valley and the archaic, Catholic, royalist *bocage* of *l'Ouest*. That contrast continued throughout the nineteenth century, but fortunately in political rather than in armed struggle.

André Siegfried, in his *Tableau politique de la France de l'Ouest sous la Troisième République*, has shown how the opposition between 'blancs' and 'bleus', 'chouans' and republicans, continued in politics long after the rebellion of the Vendéens had ended. The *départements* of the Vendée, Maine-et-Loire, Mayenne, and the west of the Sarthe were, and still are, the most solid bastions of the conservative right. That *grand seigneur*, the Vicomte de Falloux, presiding over his lands at Bourg d'Iré in the Segréen, typified one aspect of the period of Louis-Philippe and the Second Empire.

The other aspect was represented by the building of the railways, which not only speeded communications, but put the cities of the Loire Valley within such easy reach of the capital that they lost a certain part of their local flavour. They destroyed the shipping traffic on the river, which earlier in the century had increased with the adoption of Mississipi-style steamboats.

They also affected the development of the region in a more subtle way. For two separate main lines were built to serve *l'Ouest*. One ran along the Loire itself to Nantes. The other ran fifty miles further north, through Le Mans and Laval to Rennes. The result was that Anjou and Maine, so often associated since their union under the Plantagenets, were now effectively separated.

The region was the scene of many battles during the later stages of the Franco-Prussian War. While Paris was under siege, a delegation of the government established itself at Tours. Meanwhile at Coulmiers, ten miles west of Orléans, a newly-raised 'Armée de la Loire' inflicted the first defeat on the Germans. But the hopes raised by this success were dashed by further severe battles, culminating in a four-day struggle outside Le Mans early in 1871. There are numerous memorials of these engagements scattered over the countryside.

The role of the Loire during the Second World War was more important still. From June 10th to 13th 1940 Tours once again became the seat of government. Winston Churchill's two dramatic flying visits to Paul Reynaud during the Battle of France took place in the Loire Valley. The first was to near Briare: the second, on June 13th, to Tours. In the Préfecture at Tours a burn on an expensive desk is still pointed out with pride as where he laid his cigar in the absence of an ashtray.

As the government retreated to Bordeaux, the Loire became the front line. The miracle was that even at that late stage, it held for forty-eight hours. The courage of the young cadets of the School of Cavalry at Saumur was one of several heroic episodes.

But by June 21st the Wehrmacht was everywhere streaming south from the river, and the towns of the Loire had paid dearly for the brief delay. Gien, Orléans, Blois, Tours and Saumur had all suffered extensive bombardment. Further damage was inflicted by Allied air-raids, and again during the liberation.

Now, however, the fertility of the Garden of France has enabled it to recover from this as from the far longer, if less fierce wars of Plantagenêt and Valois, and it is time to see it as it is today.

The

APPROACHES

Now, with some knowledge of the landscape which makes up the region, and of its historical background, you are ready to approach it. In these penny-pinching times (and petrol has always been expensive in France) you will want to get full value from every gallon by noting everything of interest along the route, and by not following the same route twice.

So I shall describe in turn the various approaches to the Loire, across *bocage* and *gâtine*, and across or beside *rivières*, before concluding with the classic journey along the river itself.

These approaches divide themselves naturally between the different Channel ports from which they lead: Calais, Dieppe, Le Havre, Cherbourg or St Malo. But they also divide naturally between the two great dynasties which once used them: the first three described here are those used by the Valois, and the remainder are those used earlier by the Plantagenets.

I
By the Nationale Sept

It is not generally realised that for fifty miles the classic 'road to the sun' runs beside the Loire. Classic because there have always been several other ways of getting to the Côte d'Azur. Classic too, because as a means of getting there quickly it has now been superseded by the Autoroute du Sud.

But a classic it will remain, because it was the route best known to the first three generations of motorists, and in particular to those writers who settled in France between the Wars: Scott Fitzgerald; Ernest Hemingway, on the move from Paris to Burgundy, or even

further south; Cyril Connolly, who wrote: 'Peeling off the kilometres to the tune of "Blue Skies", sizzling down the long black
liquid reaches of Nationale Sept, the plane trees going sha-sha-sha
through the open window, the windscreen yellowing with crushed
midges . . . '

It is a classic right from the start, sweeping past the ultra-modern
but essentially Gallic complex of blocks and levels which constitutes
Orly Airport, and before the very gates of the older but equally
Gallic complex of wings and levels which constitutes the Palace of
Fontainebleau. Then as it leaves the Forest of Fontainebleau it
joins the Loing, only a few miles from where this little river flows
into the Seine.

The Loing occupies what was once the bed of the Loire itself,
before this turned west, and so its valley provides the lowest route
between Loire and Seine, and the course for the canal joining these
two *fleuves*. Road, river and canal are fascinatingly intertwined.

To experience this complexity, veer left from the Nationale Sept
at Montargis for twenty-five miles over the bare Gâtinais. This, as
its name indicates, is poor country similar to the *gâtines* further
west. The one halt of interest along it is at La Bussière, where a
Museum of Fishing has been set up in a seventeenth-century
château surrounded by a moat and a lake.

A parallel, minor road takes you past Montbouy, with some
Roman remains I have never been able to locate, to Châtillon-
Coligny. This owes the second part of its name to the great Protestant family of the Wars of Religion. The Admiral de Coligny, the
most eminent victim of the Massacre of St Bartholomew, lies buried
at the foot of the vast sixteen-sided keep. The only remnant of the
château which dates from his own lifetime is a well attributed to
Jean Goujon, the sculptor of the school of Fontainebleau, set amidst
the terraces above the Loing.

It is several million years since this valley was the course of the
Loire – time enough for the smaller successor stream to have worn
itself a deeper, narrower bed. This causes a significant difference in
level at the point where the canal leaves that bed to follow the water-
less stretch of the former Loire valley not borrowed by the Loing.

The change occurs at the quiet village of Rogny, the French
equivalent of Foxton, where seven stone-built locks climb steeply
in succession from the level of the Loing up to that of the old Loire.
As a combined engineering and architectural achievement they

would be remarkable in any age. It comes therefore as a surprise to learn that they were built under Henri IV, two generations earlier than Colbert's justly-famed Canal du Midi. They were last used in 1842, since when the canal has taken a slightly different course, with seven rather less dramatic locks.

The Loire itself, like the Loing, has continued to eat away its new valley, so when the canal reaches it at Briare it again finds itself at a much higher level. Here it solves the problem by crossing it on a stone bridge more than a mile long. Built in the 1890s, it is the largest of its kind in the world.

Walking across this bridge, beneath its cast-iron *art nouveau* lamp standards, you have a dramatic first view of the Loire. It is quite a typical stretch, with a sandy *plage* outside the little town, and the flat Sologne stretching to the horizon from the further shore.

All it lacks is a château, the trademark most closely associated with the river. For that you have to turn aside ten miles earlier from the Nationale Sept – which you rejoined at Briare – to take the N 140. This is one of the loveliest and least-known main roads of France, running through rich Berry and lonely Limousin, and only ending deep in the south-west at Figeac on the Lot. Follow it now, though, only as far as the Loire, which it crosses at Gien.

Again there is a *plage*, with a particularly well equipped camp site adding a touch of blue and white to the further bank. Gien is a rather large town, with a long line of shops and cafés facing the road along the quayside. This is a feature with which you will become increasingly familiar with visits to the more important centres downstream.

But the most important feature is the château. Its flat façade of red and white bricks forming a diamond pattern dominates Gien from a hill rising steeply from the *quais*, giving little hint of the restoration it has received since it and much of the town were badly damaged in the battles on the Loire in June 1940.

Built at the end of the fifteenth century by Anne de Beaujeu, the thin-lipped but capable daughter of Louis XI, who as Regent maintained the royal authority for her young brother Charles VIII, it has sheltered François I and Louis XIV. Today it houses an International Museum of Shooting, illustrated both by weapons and in pictures, including a hundred by Louis XIV's own painter of game, François Desportes.

It is not an association with Valois or Bourbon royalty which led to Gien's selection as a home for this museum. Their speciality was not *la chasse à tir* – shooting, but *la chasse à courre* – hunting. The reason was the nearness of the Sologne, where each October, in countless shooting lodges, Desportes's *natures mortes* are re-created crowded with slaughtered *gibier* and *volaille*.

It was at Gien that Joan of Arc both began and ended her four months' stay in the Loire Valley, which changed the history of Europe. Here, on March 1st 1429, her party first reached the river on their way from Vaucouleurs. After the mounting drama of the interview at Chinon, the relief of Orléans, and the victories of Patay and Jargeau, she returned this way with the Dauphin at the end of June on the way to his coronation at Reims. The pleasing modern, Romanesque-inspired church of Ste-Jeanne d'Arc beside the château has only inherited a square tower from an earlier building where Joan herself worshipped.

Gien is the natural place from which anyone travelling up or down the Valley heads off north or east. Five and a half centuries later I automatically chose the post office on Gien *quai* as the address for my mail to await me while I interrupted my Loire journeyings for a sortie into Burgundy. It is also the ideal departure point for a journey down the river. For Gien is not only the first mentioned, but *the* first *château de la Loire*, in the sense of being furthest upstream.

For this very reason, this seems the appropriate chapter in which to follow the Nationale Sept beside the Loire until it deserts it for the Allier. Although no longer an 'approach', this runs along the frontier region, where the hills of Burgundy crowd ever closer to the right bank, until at Nevers you are almost within sight of the Morvan, the nearest mountainous district to Paris.

Burgundy means wine. Vineyards reappear on both sides of this section of the Loire, after a long gap from Meung. Once grapes were grown all along the 'bend' up to and down from Orléans, but improvements in transport have killed the local *vins ordinaires* and spared only superior vintages. Such is Pouilly-Fumé on the right bank, and so too are the equally celebrated growths of Sancerre on the left.

It is not only in its dry white wines that Sancerre is always a discovery. The hills of the Sancerrois come as a surprise after the level country to the west, as does the higgledy-piggledy stone-built little town after the undistinguished brick and plaster hamlets of the

Sologne. It has a château with a fifteenth-century keep, and a ruined church tower. But of greater architectural interest is the immense Gothic choir of St-Satur at the bottom of the hill, nearer the river.

Sancerre can be reached from a side road off the Nationale Sept. But many will prefer to travel from Gien or Briare on the less frequented road along the left bank. This contrast between a quieter but slower road to the south of the Loire, and a busier highway to the north, is one often seen elsewhere further downstream. Over many stretches the conscientious visitor must take both if he is not to miss much of interest. But on this stretch, though not on all, you can keep to the less exhausting road, crossing on long bridges to places of interest on the right bank.

There are two here. Cosne is a pleasing market town with two mediaeval churches. La Charité-sur-Loire has a vast Romanesque church, left by a former abbey which was the origin, and for many centuries the livelihood of the little town. Odd monastic buildings, adapted to other uses, can be found up and down the older streets. You may be as lucky as I was one June day, when I found a courteous and well-informed student who had devoted part of his vacation to exploring this ancient foundation, and showing visitors its hidden beauties.

After La Charité white Charollais cattle take the place of vines. Their home country is sixty miles to the south-east. But their breeders, seeing the rich pastures of the Nivernais on their way to and from Paris, have taken to sending their fatstock here immediately before despatching it to market.

The Nationale Sept crosses the Loire at Nevers, four miles upstream from the junction with its dominating tributary, the Allier. Maurice Genevoix, himself of the Loire, gives three reasons why it does not bear instead the name Allier. In the first place, though the Allier often appears larger, its average flow is less: ninety cubic metres a second against a hundred and twenty-five. It is also shorter than the upper Loire: four hundred and ten kilometres against four hundred and thirty. And above all it is the Loire, not the Allier, which since the first human migrations has provided the shortest and most direct route from the shores of Provence to the plains around Paris.

Nevers, capital of the *département* of the Nièvre, and of the ancient province of the Nivernais, is undeservedly little visited. It is just the right size to have benefited from, without being spoiled by, France's postwar industrial expansion. Its 40,000-odd inhabitants have a fine *plage* on the river, and a magnificent new *Maison de la Culture* on the opposite bank. Yet its towers and gables still give it a mediaeval skyline.

However, there is a very unmediaeval cleanliness about its squares and monuments. These include the Cathedral, in styles ranging from Roman foundations to a fifteenth-century choir; the Romanesque jewel of St-Étienne; the fourteenth-century Porte de Croux; the early seventeenth-century Chapel of the Visitation; and the museum in the magnificent eighteenth-century episcopal palace. Eighteenth-century bishops everywhere went in for magnificence. But the bishops of Nevers had perhaps a better excuse than most, for their see lay in the Loire Valley.

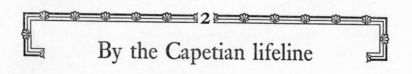

By the Capetian lifeline

The history of this region shows how the one ace of the early kings of France – other than the crown itself – was the fact that the tiny territory actually under their control straddled the middle valley of the Loire as well as the middle valley of the Seine. Orléans, in the eleventh century, was as often their residence as Paris. It could easily have become the capital of France, but instead remained the traditional seat of the junior branch of the royal family – that long series of Dukes of Orléans who gave such trouble to their seniors, right up to the very last day of the legitimist monarchy.

The road from Paris to Orléans was the lifeline of these early Capetians. Their difficulties, and their ultimate triumph, can be seen by following it.

It was a lifeline at first very much at risk. Only fifteen miles out from Paris, on the left of the road, stands the keep of Montlhéry. Its robber barons extracted a regular toll from travellers until they were dislodged by Louis VI, a far more energetic ruler than his nickname of 'the Fat' might suggest.

Soon after, at Arpajon where so many of the capital's vegetables are grown, take the opportunity of bearing left along a series of minor roads through little places like La Ferté-Alais, Courances and Milly-la-Forêt, as delightful as their names. It is an area of quite unexpected bucolic character, less than thirty miles from the Arc de Triomphe. One wonders for how long it can stay so rural, if the statisticians' projections are realised of a population for Paris by the end of the century of fourteen million. Pierre Levéel's all too plausible prophecy is that 'the entire territory of the first Capetians will form the French megalopolis'.

The main road, the N 20, runs on through Etampes with its many ancient churches, and climbs to the plateau of the Beauce. This vast cornland shares with the beetroot fields of the north the responsibility for that opinion held by so many rapidly travelling Britons that 'French landscape is so uninteresting'. They would echo the mediaeval Latin poet:

Bielsa triste solum, cui desant bis tria solum:
Fontes, prata, nemus, lapides, arbusta, racemus.

O Beauce! Thou sorry land, wanting in sixfold measure:
Springs, meadows, forests, rocks, vineyards and orchards,
All are lacking in thy treasure.

Yet this is '*la plaine immense*' of one of Victor Hugo's loveliest lyrics, and the background to some of Millet's best-known paintings – *Le Semeur*, for example, or *L'Angélus*.

Their view was shared, moreover, by no less a figure than Rabelais's Gargantua. For when his mare knocked down the woods hereabouts, so that '*feust tout le pays reduict en campaigne*', he exclaimed, in one of the most painful puns of the sixteenth or any other century: '*je trouve beau ce*'.

The story contains a grain of truth in that Beauce was once covered by trees – the ancient Belsa forest from which it derives its name. These were cleared very early in the Middle Ages, as is shown by the ancient suffix -*ville* of so many of the villages – Baudreville, Outarville, Mereville. Any later this would have ended in -*villiers*. Later still, in the great 'internal colonisation' of the eleventh to thirteenth centuries, they would instead have had the prefix *Ville-*.

Artenay, towards the southern end of the plateau, was the site of the 'Battle of Herrings', when on February 12th 1429, an English

convoy defeated a French attempt to prevent a supply of Lenten
fish from reaching the army besieging Orléans. And soon after that
siege was lifted Joan of Arc inflicted a decisive defeat on the English
in open battle at Patay, a mere ten miles away to the west.

Patay is a typical *beauceron* village, clustered round a tall spire
on one of the swelling rises which interrupt this never totally flat
plateau. The Beauce is criss-crossed by dry valleys, only slightly
below its average level; beneath these valleys lie underground
reserves of water which make possible the rich harvests.

South from Artenay something less typically *beauceron* distin-
guishes the villages: a few trees. And then a bluish line on the
horizon suddenly materialises as extensive woodland. It is the
Forest of Orléans. 'Extensive woodland' fairly describes this area,
over forty miles long, where the Capetians hunted. With its poor,
sandy soil it could never be dense. Geographers regard this as a
northward continuation of the infertile Sologne, cut off by the
Loire when it changed its course to the west.

Like the Sologne, it has numerous small lakes where a pleasant
day can be spent picnicking. Some are quiet but hard to reach.
Others, like the Etang de la Vallée, are all too accessible and provide
such amenities as *frites* and *pédalos*.

But, unlike most of the Sologne, the Forest of Orléans contains
some notable monuments. The châteaux of Chamerolles and of
Claireau are both surrounded by moats, although the first was built
in the fourteenth century and the second under Louis XIV. The
ruins of the beautifully named Abbey of La Cour-Dieu are largely
incorporated in a private house. You cannot avoid trespassing for
fifty yards or so, and braving a few nettles, in order to penetrate
inside the roofless Cistercian church to the left of the entrance gate.

Even at its widest, the forest does not extend to a quarter of its
length. On the main N 20 from Paris you pass through it in barely
five miles, and are already on the edge of Orléans. It is a pity that
the road is almost level. For if it descended to the city from an
appreciable height it would be easier to appreciate its cornerstone
situation at the northernmost point of the Loire's course. It stands
like Genoa at the meeting point of two *rivières*. The Riviera di
Levante to the east is echoed by the Val d'Orléans, as the Loire
Valley from Orléans to Gien is often known. The Riviera di Ponente
to the west corresponds to the Val de Loire running down to Blois
and Tours.

1. *Fishing beside one of the lesser* rivières

I wish to thank the French Government Tourist Office in
London for permission to use all the photographs in this book

2

3

4

2. *Romanesque capital at St-Bénoît*   3. *Renaissance well at Châtillon-Coligny*
4. *Statue in the grounds of Madame de Pompadour's château of Ménars*

5

6

5. *Grand staircase of François I within courtyard of château of Blois*
6. *Louis XII's porcupine emblem on château of Blois*

7

8

7. *Château of Cheverny*
8. *Château of Chambord*

9

10

9. *Château of Chenonceaux*
10. *Château of Amboise illuminated*

11

12

11. *Tours Cathedral seen across the Loire*
12. *Grange de Meslay*

13

14

13. *Room where Charles VIII married Anne of Brittany in château of Langeais*
14. *Château and gardens of Villandry*

15

17

15. *Château of Azay-le-Rideau*
17. *Chinon*

16

18

16. *La Devinière : birthplace of Rabelais*
18. *The Loire where Touraine meets Anjou*

19

20

Scene from Tenture de l'Apocalypse, *château of Angers*
20. Vendanges *in front of château of Saumur*

21

22

21. *Château of Angers*
22. *Château of Le Plessis-Bourré*

23

24

23. *Wine cellars hollowed out of the tufa, beside the Loir*
24. *Château of Lassay*

In spite of its past importance as the trans-shipment point for the boats which could only come downstream as far as here, to those which were able to make their way in both directions along the Val de Loire; or as a rival to Paris in the eleventh century; or even as the very key to the kingdom in the fifteenth, it is today a smaller city than Angers, and a much smaller city than Tours. This is partly because it is so near Paris, and it may grow as the 'megalopolis' extends. Already some people commute to the capital on the fast trains from Les Aubrais.

As a result the shops of the rue Royale, the main street leading down to where there has always been a bridge over the Loire, are smaller and less specialised than those of the rue Nationale at Tours. But the city has kept more of its original character.

The Orléans of the great siege of 1429, for example, is easily recognisable in the streets to the south and west of the huge cathedral. Though it was destroyed by the Protestants, its rebuilding between 1601 and 1829 – the entire span of legitimist Bourbon rule – kept surprisingly close to its original Gothic plan. Without being a great work of art, it does manage to combine the sense of antiquity of the mediaeval with the unity of style found in the best neo-Gothic.

In the garden behind stands the former bishop's palace, now the public library, with a priceless collection of books and manuscripts inherited from the former University of Orléans and the monastery of St-Benoît.

Within the ancient city walls are a number of Renaissance houses. In one of these, now the town hall, François II, the young husband of Mary Queen of Scots, died in 1560; and his brother, Charles IX, fell in love with a young *orléanaise* named Marie Touchet.

The former town hall, the Hôtel des Creneaux, is now the Musée des Beaux-Arts. Although not in the first rank of provincial museums, it has a fine collection of French seventeenth- and eighteenth-century paintings, including a Georges de la Tour St Sebastian. A series of vast allegorical canvases illustrating the four elements with scenes from the court of Louis XIII comes from the vanished château of Richelieu. And the St Thomas of Velasquez is the painter's one absolutely authentic work in a French public collection.

Other Renaissance mansions bear such names as Maison de la Coquille, Maison de François I (his mistress the Duchesse d'Etampes once lived there) and Maison de Diane de Poitiers (no connection with her – it is now the archaeological museum).

There are several mediaeval churches both within and outside the former walls, but none are of outstanding merit. Of greater interest are two mediaeval civil buildings. The Salle des Thèses was the law library of the former University, where Jean Calvin studied between 1528 and 1533. Like all mediaeval universities on the Continent, it was divided into 'nations', institutions midway between Oxbridge colleges and American fraternities; and it is significant that in Calvin's time Lutheran ideas were active in the *nation germanique*.

The Salle des Thèses is in stone, and has therefore required less restoration than the half-timbered Maison de Jeanne d'Arc. She stayed here during the ten days when she raised the siege, and it has been filled with objects of her time or in some way associated with her.

Her most prominent monument in the city is her statue on horse-back in the centre of the square at the top of the rue Royale. It is well worth walking slowly round, to study the scenes of her career in bronze reliefs which decorate the pedestal. One is then in the right mood to go down the rue Royale, across the bridge, and to find, a little to the left, the site of the Tourelles fort. Her capture of this decided the English to raise the siege.

This is also the opportunity to visit the Municipal Rose Garden, by retracing one's steps to the end of the bridge and bearing left for about a quarter of a mile. With some ten thousand rose trees, of five hundred different varieties, this enclosure at one end of a long Botanic Garden is the city's tribute to its own nursery gardening industry.

Almost next door to the Maison de Jeanne d'Arc is another Renaissance house. It is the Musée et Centre Charles Péguy. It has photographs showing the writer and where he lived and studied; his school reports; complete series of his *Cahiers de la Quinzaine*, not only written, but also published and even distributed by himself; and details of the movements of the cavalry detachment he com-manded at the time of his death, aged 40, at the beginning of the first battle of the Marne. A special room illustrates his pilgrimages on foot between 1912 and 1914 from Paris to Notre-Dame de Chartres.

It is a delightful little museum. Yet I felt that I had to get closer still to the man himself, and to the basic spirit of Orléans in which he grew up, which has been described by René Crozet as 'severe and serious: the crude humour of the *tourangeau* wine-grower disappears but the harshness remains: it is the famous "waspish" humour, joined to the proverbial *beauceron* avarice'.

On that October night I walked east, beyond the mediaeval city, beyond its later extensions, and over a level crossing into the working-class suburb where Péguy was born in 1873. I had some trouble finding his birthplace, 48 faubourg de Bourgogne, and went into a local café to ask the way.

I was there for the rest of the evening. When I left I not only knew that he had been born at No. 48, but brought up at No. 52. I knew, too, something of the humble but happy milieu which had produced this fine man.

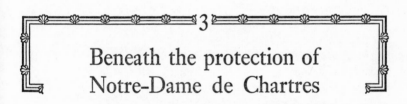

3
Beneath the protection of
Notre-Dame de Chartres

The road from Paris to Chartres is not the route of Péguy's pedestrian pilgrimage. But those who follow it come just as much beneath the mesmerising influence, and the blessing, of those twin towers which suddenly come into view above the cornfields of the Beauce. Whether you go with him into the quiet, small streets beside the placid Eure, or turn aside on to the autoroute which now bypasses the city altogether, you may feel the need to place yourself under the protection of Our Lady of Chartres, patron of the outpost of the Île de France which is also the first city of *l'Ouest*.

Unnoticed, the route crosses the watershed between Seine and Loire. Less than fifteen miles from where the Route Nationale 10 leaves the Eure it meets the Loir. This forms much of the charm of Bonneval, just off the main road, filling moats and waterways as well as its own bed. Other attractions of this neglected little town are a thirteenth-century church, and a number of buildings, dating from the eleventh to the eighteenth centuries, which once formed

a Benedictine abbey. Although these are now occupied by a psy-
chiatric hospital, one can wander all round the grounds. There is
a particularly fine abbot's lodge, whose stonework has a diamond
pattern like that on the château of Gien. It was built in 1490 by
René d'Illiers, who came from, and was named after, the next small
town upstream on the Loir. This lies on an alternative route from
Chartres to the N 10, a peaceful place, and with another attraction.

Illiers, under the name of Combray, is known throughout the
world to millions who have never even set foot in France. It is the
setting for some of the most haunting passages of *A la recherche du
temps perdu*. Marcel Proust used as a child to stay here with his
aunt, Madame Amiot. Her plain little house, opening straight on
the rue du Docteur-Proust (Marcel's father, and her brother), has
been turned into a museum filled with furniture and objects the
writer would recognise.

It is an odd experience to chat with aged residents who actually
remember Madame Amiot, or to buy at the *boulangerie* a few yards
away one of the famous *madeleines* of 'Tante Leonie', as he named
her in the book.

The *Société des amis de Marcel Proust*, who have arranged the
museum, also look after the Pré-Catalan, half a mile out along the
road to Dangeau. Formerly the property of the Amiots, this acre
or so of walks, hedges and rough lawns was used by them for
exercises and picnics. It appears in Proust's work as 'le parc de
Swann'. On my own visit it was in the charge of a friendly retired
gamekeeper, whose first-hand tales of country life in the Perche
were even more interesting than his second-hand stories about the
Proust family.

The road through Illiers and the road by Bonneval meet up again
at Châteaudun. This has a bland sound for many English ears, too
like Châteauneuf, or Châteauroux, or Châteaumeillant. But concentrate on the suffix, which gives Dunois, the name of its citizens,
and of the county of which it was once the capital. It was also the
title, conferred on him by his father, of the Duke of Orléans, Joan
of Arc's stoutest companion, 'the bastard of Orléans'.

Half the château which is the town's main monument was built
by him. It is at the point of a peninsula of high land beside the
Loir. The rest of Châteaudun stretches behind it on this gradually
widening peninsula. It was largely rebuilt on a regular street-plan
after a fire in 1723. Entering it from every direction but one is

a stiff climb, followed by the impression of a predominantly eighteenth-century town as you reach the main square, the place du 18 octobre, at the summit and centre.

Only as you go – preferably on foot – downhill towards the point of the peninsula, do you find narrower streets with older houses. The rue St-Lubin, with its stream running down the middle, explains the phrase *tenir le haut du pavé*. It had always mystified me why this should be used of anyone adopting the attitude of a superior, till one day I found out that it was only by keeping to the higher, outer edge of the cobbled mediaeval streets that the upper classes could avoid being splashed from the stinking sewer which ran down their centre.

The castle remains hidden until you suddenly stumble on it. It lies lower than the square at the top of the town, and beyond a tall gateway at the end of a street, which is a good viewpoint from which to examine it.

To the left is the fifteenth-century wing built by Dunois himself, with its attached 'Flamboyant' Gothic chapel of the same date. To the right stands the sixteenth-century, Renaissance wing. Each has a magnificent staircase in its own, quite different style. Above these is the circular keep adjoining the chapel, built in the twelfth century. Old itself, it probably occupies the site of one built by Thibault the Cheat, Count of Blois, two hundred years earlier still.

Inside, the walls of the immense rooms are covered by tapestries from the state collection, regularly changed. Those who have never developed the admittedly acquired taste for tapestries may take more pleasure from the fifteen life-size fifteenth-century statues of saints in the chapel. Half a century older than the earliest of the Saints of Solesmes, they make an interesting contrast with those of the great abbey on the Sarthe.

There is another first view of the château, seen by those arriving from Illiers, as they go down to the Loir through the *faubourg* of St Jean, which is grouped around one of Châteaudun's four medi-aeval churches. Suddenly it is there across the river, rising almost directly two hundred feet from where the peninsula of land abruptly ends. Much of this façade is just that: a facing of stone on the rock beneath. But it gives an impression of immense strength, with which the Renaissance wing which crowns it contrasts intriguingly.

The road due south from Châteaudun runs across the extremity of the corn plateau, here known as 'the little Beauce', or as *la queue*, the 'tail' of Beauce. Several of the villages have interesting churches, notably Rhodon with its frescoes, a mile off the road to the west.

From this route too, you can branch off east to visit Talcy, wholly of the Beauce although it lies only eight miles from the Loire. The military exterior of its château hides a charming Renaissance courtyard with an ornamental well, built by the Florentine Bernard Salviati. His daughter Cassandre was the first of a long line of girls to receive the admiration and to inspire the poetry of Pierre de Ronsard, who lived just over thirty miles to the west.

A generation later her niece, Diane Salviati, began here a love affair with a very different poet, the redoubtable Protestant warrior Agrippa d'Aubigné. In the following century, ironically, the château was the birthplace of Godet des Marais, Bishop of Chartres and confessor of Agrippa d'Aubigné's granddaughter. She was to become Madame de Maintenon, who persuaded her husband Louis XIV to expel the Protestants from France.

This area is the Blésois, the *pays* of Blois. Like many other ancient administrative unities, it included a variety of soils and cultivations to give it a certain autonomy. It includes parts of the Beauce, of *gâtine*, of the Val de Loire itself, and of the Sologne. Something both of the richness and of the limitations of the old self-sufficient way of life can be experienced by turning right five miles before Blois.

Superficially a very ordinary village, Marolles is remarkable because of the decision of its craftsmen, when their trades were threatened by industrial competition, to fight back by an appeal to the 'home-made' market. Workshops can be visited where furniture, pottery, and wrought-iron objects are made and sold. I was shown round them by a retired smith, who also had the key to a little museum of agricultural and village life, where he was able to point to many of the now obsolete implements as his own handiwork.

Just as interesting as what he showed me was what he told me about changes in country life. Only twenty years ago, before the *remembrement* which in one French village after another is concentrating the scattered peasant holdings into larger, easier-worked blocks of land, the farms each had their quota of vines and cattle. Now the profitable corn crop covers all; and the wine and milk drunk in Marolles come from elsewhere.

The changes are all recent. The old smith had lived and worked right up to late middle age in a society much like that of the fifteenth century. This is why the exhibits in the museum were so complete, and in such good condition. They had simply been collected from where they had recently been discarded in stable or kitchen. To assemble a similar collection in England would require the techniques almost of archaeology; many of the objects on view at Marolles have not been in use here since the nineteenth, or even the eighteenth century.

'We owe a lot to the last War', I was told by the man who showed me round the Musée des Arts et Traditions Populaires in the Bois de Boulogne. 'It acted not merely as a brake, but as an archaising influence. Between the Wars mechanisation had got very slowly under way. But when supplies of petrol and so much else were cut off in 1940, the scythes and sickles and pony-traps were still at hand in the outhouses. As a result the French countryside as it emerged in 1945 was not merely that of 1940, but that of 1920, or even that of 1900. Nor were the immediate postwar years easy. Only by about 1955 had economic recovery reached the point where modernisation could recommence. And by then there were enough of us about with an interest in preserving at least a selection of the tools and artefacts of the pre-industrial world.'

The five miles into Blois is a return to the present, but not quite all the way. Its site on a steep little range of hills above the right bank of the Loire, and its landmark of a château, are reminders of the past.

Because of this line of hills, or *coteaux*, Blois, which has the smallest population, under 50,000, of the major towns on the Loire, is at first the most confusing to find one's way around. It has two distinct centres of interest: the château itself on one hill, and the cathedral on another. It also has two equally distinct business centres. One inevitably lies along the *quais*, and around the square by the bridge over the Loire, the other round the square behind the hill on which stands the château. These two squares are joined by the main shopping street, the rue Denis Papin, which follows the break between the hills.

Denis Papin was born at Chitenay across the river in 1647. His statue stands halfway up a staircase climbing the *coteau* from this street. It was he who revealed to the world the force of steam power. In 1707, in exile in Germany as a Protestant, he even experimented with a steamboat. But apart from the earliest type of pressure cooker, still known as a *marmite de Papin*, no practical application of his theories was made until later.

The château is entered from an airy square on top of the hill, with plenty of parking space. Blois has more visitors than any other château in the Loire Valley. You may have to wait a while with thirty or so companions to be allocated to a guide and begin your tour.

Blois was also visited by Joan of Arc on her way to the relief of Orléans. Of the château she knew there remains only the thirteenth-century Salle des États, where the States General met twice under Henri III. It makes less impression from within the courtyard than the three famous wings which make this building so important in the history of French architecture.

The first, that of Louis XII, together with the chapel, is late Gothic. The recurring motifs of porcupine and ermine are those of Louis XII and his Queen, Anne of Brittany.

The second wing, that of François I, although only a dozen years younger, is wholly of the Renaissance. Here the distinguishing badge is the salamander, as enigmatic as François's own eyes, yet of the same compelling fascination. The magnificent Grand Staircase is set in an octagonal tower which is almost like lacework in stone.

The third was constructed between 1635, when Gaston d'Orléans, the intrigue-loving younger brother of Louis XIII, was exiled from court, and 1638, when his allowance was drastically cut by Richelieu; if this had not happened, the wings of François I and of Louis XII would in their turn have been demolished to make way for a less interesting classical palace.

The wing has been much criticised; by Henry James, for example: 'As one stands in the court of the castle, and lets one's eye wander from the splendid wing of François I – which is the last work of free and joyous invention – to the ruled lines and blank spaces of the ponderous pavilion of Mansard, one makes one's reflections upon the advantage, in even the least personal of the arts, of having something to say . . .'

The design, by François Mansart (inventor of the Mansard roof) is a model of its period, but its unfinished staircase ending in a two-storeyed dome is unique. The wing which it replaced was that of Charles d'Orléans, the poet-duke who established a brilliant court at Blois on his return from imprisonment in England in 1440. His son made the château his home both before and after he became King Louis XII, and his Queen, Anne of Brittany, died here. During the lifetime of their daughter Claude, who married François I, it remained one of the main royal residences. It was still used occasionally by his son and grandsons right up to the tragic meeting of the States General summoned here by Henri III, when he arranged the murder of the two elder Guise brothers.

The scenes of these assassinations, and in particular that of the Duke of Guise himself, form the most dramatic part of the tour. You are shown, perhaps with a little too much certainty, the route he took, where the lurking *mignons* began to stab him, where he finally died, and where the King had been waiting.

Equally haunting is the room where Henri III's mother, Catherine de Médicis, died a few days later. It was at a ball at the château, too, that Ronsard first met Cassandre Salviati of Talcy. Nowhere in France does one feel closer to the later Renaissance.

The first floor of the Louis XII wing houses the Musée des Beaux-Arts which every departmental capital has. English visitors will be particularly interested in an *Execution of Thomas More* by a French artist. On the ground floor is a National Museum of Religious Art.

Blois is an appropriate place for such a national museum, as it has three churches of considerable but very different architectural interest. The oldest, St Nicolas, just below the château towards the Loire, was built between the twelfth and thirteenth centuries, so that the choir and transept are Transitional, and the nave is Gothic. The marriage of styles is a total success.

The cathedral, on the hill to the east, was rebuilt after its destruction by a hurricane in 1678, but in an odd seventeenth-century Gothic, even stranger than that of Orléans.

Notre-Dame de la Trinité, half a mile further east along the *coteau*, was finished in 1939. But it would be imaginative if built today, with its cement statues, its modern stained-glass windows, and its tower with no less than forty-five bells. Modern architects often design good crypts, as at Lourdes. Here there are two.

On the cathedral hill are a number of well preserved mediaeval and Renaissance houses. Behind the cathedral stands the former bishop's palace, built early in the eighteenth century by Jacques Gabriel. Its gardens provide one of the best of all the views of the river, and you will no doubt agree with Henry James in a friendlier mood: 'Blois has that aspect of cheerful leisure which belongs to all white towns that reflect themselves in shining waters.'

On the left, a couple of miles upstream, a dam has created an artificial lake. The 'leisure complex' being built around this already includes camp sites and a sailing school. Beyond the Loire lie the forests of the Sologne which shelter the game once hunted from Cheverny and Chambord.

By the Maine road

The Angevin Empire of Henry II stretched all the way from Ireland to the Pyrenees. But its heart lay between the Channel and the Loire: in Anjou, Maine and Normandy.

These were the provinces he had inherited or conquered before the death of Stephen gave him England, or his marriage with Eleanor extended his influence over the South-West. In leaving Normandy to cross Maine, you are following the route which he or his emissaries must often have taken on their way to or from England. It is also the most convenient route to the Loire from the Norman ports of Dieppe or Le Havre.

Throughout the journey the countryside is very different from the endless bare Beauce across which the approaches from the east run. Here a mere eighty miles take you from one of the most 'raw' climates of the country to *le jardin de la France*, through a succession of revealing landscapes.

The climate of the Orne is raw because this southernmost department of Normandy stands high. Where not covered by immense forests like those of Andaine and Écouves, it is largely devoted to the breeding of horses.

But the highest point of all, highest in fact in the entire *Ouest*, lies just over the frontier in Maine. To find an altitude greater than the 1390 feet of the Mont des Avaloirs one needs to go all the way to the Belgian border or to Burgundy. The flat forest does not convey a sense of great height to anyone actually there. It is only a raised platform which provides a commanding view of these mountainous marches between the provinces.

'Mountainous' is a relative term. Snowdonia or the Grampians are hills compared with the Himalayas. But the Alpes Mancelles, seven miles south-east of the Mont des Avaloirs, are a sixth of Ben Nevis, just as Ben Nevis is a sixth of Everest. Nevertheless, these gorse- and bramble-covered rocks, like the Derbyshire Peak District, have a certain Alpine quality. It would be a pity to miss them.

They can be seen with the least deviation from the route by leaving the Orne on the little Route Départementale 505. This is a continuation of the road south from Carrouges, a useful meeting-place of roads from the Channel.

There are two early advantages. The first is the primitive pilgrimage chapel of Ste-Anne, just before Champfrémont. The building is uninteresting, but the grass, shady trees, and chairs and tables provide, as once or twice a year they do for the pilgrims, an ideal place for a picnic. The second is the view from Ste-Anne of the Mont des Avaloirs, like a menacing low black cloud, made even more sinister by the dull green of the Forest of Multonne which covers its side.

The road descends through two pretty villages with the picturesque names of St-Pierre-des-Nids and St-Céneri-le-Gerei. The church of the second has fine mediaeval frescoes. There is also a chapel dedicated to St Céneri, a seventh-century Italian hermit whose brother settled in an equally lovely valley forty miles south-west, at Saulges.

The river which curls round St-Céneri is the Sarthe. Although it rises in the Orne, and for many miles is the frontier between Normandy and Maine, it belongs by right to the *département* called after it, which you now enter over an old bridge. The passage which the river carves through the Alpes Mancelles gives them much of their attraction.

This gorge has turned the next village, St-Léonard-des-Bois, into an inland resort. It is not crowded, but those wanting a quiet stay, with good walks by the river and by the Romanesque church of St-Léonard, up the surrounding hills, or along the wild Vallée de Misère, will find here a camp site, a swimming pool, and an excellent *Logis de France*.

Geologically the Alpes Mancelles are a northward extension of the Coëvrons, a ridge running across Maine from south-west to north-east. The name of these beginnings of the Breton hill country is suitably Celtic. *Coët* means wood, and *vron* breast. The heights surrounding Sillé-le-Guillaume, the other inland resort of this area, do resemble 'wooded breasts'. It is lucky in having this vast forest, as well as a lake round which there are a camp site, hotel, sailing school, riding club and tennis courts. The little town, a couple of miles from the lake, has a château (now a college) once captured by William the Conqueror, with a keep a hundred and twenty-five feet high.

This route, though, goes not through Sillé but through Fresnay-sur-Sarthe, a little fortified town with a fine old Romanesque church, which was also twice captured by him. Like many of the larger villages in the Sarthe, it is classified as a *Station verte de Vacances*. This scheme for attracting holidaymakers to the country-side by providing them with amenities began in this department, and it still has its national head office in Le Mans.

Beaumont-sur-Sarthe, eight miles further on than Fresnay, has much the same charm and history. Two villages just off this stretch have a special interest. The absentee vicar of St-Christophe-du-Jambet, on the right, was once Rabelais.

Vivoin, to the left, has a Benedictine priory, complete with church, thirteenth-century chapter house, prior's lodge and court-room. It has been rescued from ruin by the local elementary school-master, who with young volunteers has restored the buildings and adapted them for use as a *Maison des Jeunes et de la Culture*; one of the outstanding achievements of the movement, which has been spearheaded and coordinated by Pierre de la Garde in his radio programme *Chefs d'Oeuvre en Péril*.

At Beaumont the route joins the main road from Alençon to Le Mans, which runs straight across the countryside in a way it could never achieve a few miles west in the Coëvrons, and some distance away from the quiet Sarthe, crossing it at St-Marceau by an old bridge with a chapel in the middle. Soon road and river alike are entering Le Mans.

The capital of the Sarthe, and former capital of Maine, is a depressing city both to enter and to stay in for any length of time. It grew unplanned from 15,000 inhabitants in 1850 to over ten times that number today. Gaunt 'HLM' (*habitations à loyer modeste*, reasonably-priced housing in austere high-rise blocks) and vast hypermarkets spoil the edges of almost every French town of any size. But in the case of Le Mans these have been extended, and rendered untidy as well as dull, by miles of cheap, unimaginative villas, each with its plot or garden. As a result it covers an area as large as that of Lyon.

This might be forgiven if there had been a parallel development of the centre, to make it a *grande ville* in amenities as well as merely in size. But there is a noticeable lack of big hotels or pleasant cafés.

Few visitors need worry about what Paul Wagret calls '*un manque d'ambiance*'. It may trouble the businessman, visiting the tractor and engine divisions of Renault or one of the four major insurance companies which unexpectedly have their head offices in Le Mans. Certainly it will shock the *assistant* or *assistante* on a year's exchange teaching, who lands up at some bleak institution in the *manceaux* suburbs. But visitors will be glad they came, if only to see the monuments.

Most of these, conveniently, are in a single small area. This narrow hill above the Sarthe formed the site of the original Gallic settlement, and later of the city which the Romans withdrew to and fortified after the first barbarian invasions of the third century. The fortifications are still largely intact, and form the oldest and largest of all the constructions of 'Le vieux Mans', the hill they surround. They still show a geometric pattern of bricks and differently-coloured stones, and half of the thirty or so semi-circular towers which originally completed the defences are still standing.

The second oldest and second largest monument is the cathedral, whose apse has replaced the Gallo-Roman wall at one corner. Added to in every century from the eleventh to the fifteenth, it consists mainly of a Romanesque nave and a Gothic choir. Each has the decoration of these styles: sculpture on the façade of the nave, and stained-glass windows in the choir and its dozen chapels. There are also stained-glass windows in the nave, which are among the few from the twelfth century to have survived in France. The tomb of Charles IV d'Anjou, Count of Maine, is the oldest Renaissance sculpture in the country. Both inside and outside, the cathedral gives an impression of immense but disorganised power.

The narrow streets of the old town are lined with fifteenth- and sixteenth-century houses which are being carefully restored to a strict over-all plan. They are becoming once again the homes of the well-to-do, for whom they were originally built. It is worth sparing the time to walk along every one of these old streets. There are three very different buildings which should not be missed. The Renaissance 'House of Adam and Eve' is so called from the faces of a man and a woman carved above the door. The eighteenth-century town hall stands on the site of the palace of the Counts of Maine. The fifteenth-century half-timbered 'Maison de la Reine Bérengère', with two attractive courtyards, is now a museum of local art, above all of pottery.

Queen Bérengère, or Berengaria as she is known in England, has her tomb in the cathedral. She was the widow of Richard Coeur-de-Lion. She had married him in an incident as romantic as any in his life, when on his way to Palestine he visited her family's kingdom of Cyprus. His death in 1199, and John's loss of most of the Plantagenet dominions in France only five years later, left her without either position or home.

Philip Augustus showed kindness but also statesmanship in granting Le Mans to his enemy's widow. She was a difficult woman, unlikely to help in any schemes of reconquest of her brother-in-law, who had inherited all the less attractive elements of the Angevin character.

Three buildings she knew still stand in the lower part of the city, though they have been added to and changed in the intervening seven and a half centuries. The former abbey church of Notre-Dame de la Couture stands beside the Préfecture, which has taken over the eighteenth-century monastic buildings. Most of it is Romanesque, but much of its roof has the fine Angevin vaulting which across the Channel is called Early English. There is a lovely white marble Virgin by the Renaissance sculptor Germain Pilon, whose name is inappropriately attached to one of the most notorious streets of Pigalle (the Paris red-light district, itself named after a sculptor).

Even more Angevin in every sense is the church of Ste-Jeanne d'Arc, further away in the same direction. It was founded as an *hôpital* or almshouse by Henry II himself in 1180, and resembles the hospital of St Jean built at the same time at Angers.

Notre-Dame-du-Pré across the Sarthe is entirely Romanesque, but the church most closely associated with Queen Berengaria lies three miles away, on the edge of the modern city. She founded the Cistercian abbey of l'Épau in 1229 beside the Huisne, the river whose junction with the Sarthe at Le Mans was part of the town's *raison d'être*. The church is vast, white and simple, as the Order preferred. The magnificent late fourteenth-century roof timbers replace those burned by the townspeople during an English siege in the Hundred Years War.

The chapter house and *scriptorium* have particularly fine vaulting. The cloister has disappeared, but the space it occupied still seems designed for visitors to gather in while waiting for their guided tour to begin. Berengaria was buried here, although her tomb is now in the cathedral.

Another, far more important Angevin tomb has been moved out of the cathedral. It is now the most important exhibit of the Musée de Tessée, in a pleasant public garden opposite and housing pictures by Georges de la Tour, Poussin, Boucher, Géricault and Constable, which by themselves would be worth a long detour. But here also is the tomb of Geoffrey Plantagenet himself, ancestor of the whole dynasty, and whose son Henry II was born at Le Mans in 1133.

Geoffrey's picture is about half life-size in coloured enamel. Despite his military achievements, I had somehow never thought of him as a soldier. It came as a surprise to find him in chain mail and helmet, like an enlarged figure from the Bayeux tapestry. His helmet was important; for it was the branch of broom, *genêt*, on it, which gave the dynasty its name.

The style of the portrait is as archaic as its subject's dress. 1150 was nearer to 1066 than to the later thirteenth and fourteenth centuries in terms of which most people think of the Middle Ages. The early Plantagenets lived in a simpler world than that of the later Valois. They moved like gypsies from one draughty castle to another, in order to 'live off their own', to eat up the supplies of their scattered estates. They were accompanied not only by their entire court and retinue, but by the primitive furnishings – rugs, wall hangings, and the wooden chests which contained their silver plate and parchment documents – which were set up in one after another of their empty residences.

The long convoy must often have crawled south from Le Mans towards Tours. If they could only have visited the scene on a June day eight centuries later, it would have appealed to the competitive, fast-riding Plantagenets. This road, closed to other traffic for a weekend, forms half the circuit of the great '24 heures du Mans', the gruelling motor race which attracts over 300,000 spectators.

These spectators, too, are likely to be satisfied with their visit to the city. The interior of the track contains, during that weekend, every amenity: restaurants, post office and even a chapel. The camp

site there, though classed as only fourth category, is available free
all the year round. Also open throughout the year is a Motor
Museum with a good collection of vintage cars, motorcycles and
bicycles. These include some of the models of Amédée Bollée, a
native of Le Mans, who invented a steam-propelled car in 1873.
His sons Léon and Amédée pioneered further developments, giving
the city every right to be a centre of interest for the automobile
industry.

Beyond the race track is the sparse countryside of the *pays
manceau*. The soil is poor and the holdings small, giving only a
meagre subsistence. This is even more the case, in many people's
view, in the plateaux to the south and east of Le Mans than in the
north and west of Maine, which have so much in common with
Brittany. Zola's grim *La Terre* was written at Cloyes-sur-le-Loir,
even further east, near Châteaudun. People from more prosperous
départements, however, say that it is in Mayenne rather than in
Sarthe that they run up against difficulties of communication in
what seems to them an altogether more primitive world.

Mechanisation came late to the agriculture of these regions. The
Sarthe had only sixteen tractors in 1917, as against twelve thousand
in 1963. They may have been less necessary here, for the most
famous products of these little farms are the *poulardes*, or fat
chickens of Maine, which are almost as well known as those of
Bresse. And on vast stretches between Le Mans and the Loir the
sandy soils have been planted with the labour-saving and profitable
pine.

There is one genuine, natural forest, with not only pines, but also
the most beautifully shaped oaks in France. The forty to sixty years
between planting and replanting of pines may seem a long time, but
it is a fraction of the two-hundred-and-sixteen-year cycle of the oaks
in the Forêt de Bercé. This is criss-crossed by ruler-straight *allées*,
along most of which visitors are allowed to drive. Two spots, the
Fontaine de la Coudre and the Source de l'Hermitage, add the
sound of running water to the sight of soaring trees, but most
interesting of all is the eighteen-acre section of the Futaie des Clos,
whose trees are never cut. The severed base of the mighty Boppe
oak is famous, though its age was two hundred and sixty-two years,
and not five hundred as is sometimes said, when it was struck by
lightning in 1934.

The Futaie des Clos is ten miles off the main road. Having got

so far, it would be a pity not to go on another six miles out of the
forest to St-Fraimbault. Its tiny church has a pre-Romanesque
choir of the ninth and tenth centuries, to which a nave was added
in the eleventh. The frescoes inside are of the fourteenth. The little-
visited Renaissance château of La Chenuère nearby has an enormous
variety of trees in its deer park.

From here it would be easier to rejoin the direct route by the
valley of the Loir, to which the main road in any case descends after
leaving the forest. A couple of miles before the river it goes through
Château-du-Loir, a pleasant white little town of no great interest
except for its confusing name. It confused me, and the friend to
whom this book is dedicated, when late one afternoon in July 1948
we decided to take a train on from Chartres to some smaller place
for the night, We were bound for the Loire Valley, which we
already knew was famous for its châteaux. So what could make a
better start for our exploration than Château-du-Loir itself? It
seemed strange that we had never heard of it before, but the railway
plan we were studying did not show rivers, and we assumed that
an 'e' had been left off the 'Loire'.

The station on the branch line from Chartres to Saumur, where
we got out late at night, is a long mile from the centre. Although the
hotel, which had stayed open for the arrival of our train, still stands,
it charges rather more than the one hundred francs (one new franc)
each we paid for our rooms. My diary tells me that next morning
'We walked into the country a little: every house had carved into
the "tufa" behind a "cave", where one had sheltered from bombs
during the war, and where now one kept wine.' No doubt we had
wandered as far as Coëmont, just before the bridge over the Loir.
Here for the first time this guide meets troglodyte dwellings, widespread along the Loir and throughout Touraine.

Another three miles and the road enters Touraine, or more precisely the *département* of Indre-et-Loire which has succeeded it. It
is better to enter it on the side-road from Dissay through St-
Christophe-sur-le-Nais and St-Paterne-Racan. Both these centres
of a small fruit-growing area have interesting churches.

The little valley here becomes narrower, and is suddenly almost
blocked by the château of la Roche-Racan. Its white walls and its
high terraces rise straight from the road, but it cannot be visited.
Its builder and first resident, Honorat de Bueil, Baron of Racan,
wrote pastoral poetry which earned him a place in the Académie

Française at its foundation in 1635. The de Bueils, like the Bouci-
cauts, were one of the great families supporting the French cause
in Touraine during the Hundred Years War.

The main road is rejoined at Neuillé-Pont-Pierre, where it is
crossed by a most useful cross-country route which runs all the way
from Blois to Seiches, only twelve miles from Angers. All who
relish the absurd will enjoy a modern stained-glass window in the
church of Neuillé showing St Martin of Tours arranging the
Armistice of 1918.

The main road runs on across typical poor *gâtine*. Semblançay
stands a mile off to the right, famous less for the ruins of its tenth- to
thirteenth-century castle than for the man known to history by the
title he derived from it. Jacques de Beaune, Baron of Semblançay,
Surintendant des Finances under Louis XII and François I, was
hanged at the age of seventy in 1527 for robbing the treasury. (The
judgement was later – too late – reversed.)

The Valley is now coming closer, approached along the narrow
main street of La Membrolle, congested with the traffic from Laval
and St Malo, then past one of the new out-of-town hypermarkets
dotted round Tours, and through the featureless suburb of St-Cyr.
A still more important junction, this time with the Nationale 10
from Chartres and Paris, and you come to the top of a steep hill,
with a magnificent eighteenth-century bridge at its base, and the
city of St Martin spread out across the river.

But the exploration of Tours itself is better described at the end
of the final approach to the valley it dominates.

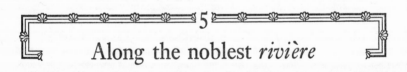

5
Along the noblest *rivière*

The Plantagenets often visited their Capetian rivals in Paris. Feudal
protocol obliged them to do so, for technically they were the French
kings' vassals although far more powerful than them. They had
other reasons. Even as long ago as the twelfth century Paris was the
city of Western Europe most worth visiting. With Suger it was the

centre of the *avant-garde* in architecture, with Abelard of the most daring advances in philosophy, with Chrétien de Troyes of the most striking developments in literature.

A visit to Paris could even have for the Angevins the same erotic lure that it did for the Victorians. On one visit, in 1151, the young Henry II, accompanying his father Geoffrey, formed that attachment with Queen Eleanor which led to her divorce the following year from Louis VII. On another visit a generation later, Richard Coeur-de-Lion fell in love with the same king's daughter. But when he asked his father for permission to make what might seem a most suitable marriage alliance, Henry II refused it on the grounds that he had himself had an affair with the girl on his own last visit to the French capital.

One of the pleasantest routes for them between Paris and their power base was the valley of the Loir. The earliest section of this route, to Chartres and the upper Loir as far as Châteaudun, has already been described. Travelling on, you can avoid altogether the busy and monotonous Nationale 10 by taking the right bank through the little walled town of Montigny-le-Ganelon, with its château restored by that ornament to French literature, the Duke of Lévis-Mirepoix.

Crossing the crowded highway to Spain at Cloyes, where Zola wrote *La Terre*, you can visit Romilly-sur-Aigre, another little fortified town, where the action of the novel takes place, before continuing along the left bank by tiny but quiet roads. Areines (i.e. 'arenas') marks the site of the Roman city which preceded the town of Vendôme, which now lies on the other bank.

The name has echoes: the Place Vendôme at Paris, with its salons of *haute couture* and its column; and the activities of more than one Duke of Vendôme in the seventeenth and eighteenth centuries. But one hardly expects such elegance and style to be reflected in the little *sous-préfecture* which gave the square its name and the dukes their title.

It was with surprise and delight therefore that I first entered it on my way to quite another part of France. All thoughts of where I had intended to get to by lunchtime were discarded as I wandered round the streets, squares and bridges. For the four or five branches of the Loir – the number depends on how you count them – give it the air of a miniature Venice, though with fewer palaces and more gardens.

Just beyond the first branch of the Loir are the church of the Madeleine and the chapel of St Jacques. Both are mainly late Gothic. In a square right in the middle of the town stands the Tower of St Martin, the remaining part of a church of the same period.

The main church is that of the abbey, La Trinité. With its former monastic buildings it still dominates a full quarter of the little town. It successfully combines every style from the Romanesque of the transept, dating from soon after its foundation by Geoffrey Martel in 1035, up to the Flamboyant façade which is later than 1500. There are fine fourteenth-century stained-glass windows in the choir. The twelfth-century bell tower stands by itself to the west, acting both as a keep and belfry, and is nearly 270 feet high. On its south side is the former cloister, close under the great nave, the chapter house and a pleasant local museum.

I remember the welcome I received at that museum one autumn evening, when by chance I met a group gathering for an adult education class in English. After chatting with them I emerged into the darkness of the vast square named after Rochambeau, the Marshal of France, born at Vendôme, who even more than Lafayette helped the Americans to victory in their War of Independence.

I remember too the walk next morning down the deserted rue de l'Abbaye on the other side of the church, to the point where part of the old fortifications spans one of the branches of the Loir. Another interesting relic of these is the Porte St-Georges, defending one of the bridges across the main branch of the river.

The ruined mediaeval château stands on a rise on the other bank. Around it lies a pleasant public garden, giving the best view of the town as a whole.

The Bourbons were Counts, and then Dukes, of Vendôme before they became Kings of France. Perhaps it is significant that the first and most popular of those kings gave the Duchy of Vendôme to the son, César, given him by his best loved mistress, Gabrielle d'Estrées, a native of Touraine. Her death in 1599, just when she was about to become his wife and his Queen, precisely marks the end of the great age of the Loire Valley.

This is a very French corner of France. As a popular song put it at the height of the English successes in the early fifteenth century:

Maintenant que reste-t-il
A ce dauphin si gentil?

Orléans, Beaugency,
Notre-Dame de Cléry.
Vendôme!
Vendôme!

The road along the Loir continues on the right bank, from which you can see the château of the Rochambeaux (not open to the public) across the valley. Do not waste time as I did at Le Gué-du-Loir (*gué* means ford) looking for the manor of La Bonaventure. Little remains of it. And the legend linking it with Antoine de Bourbon and Ronsard is just that, for the *gué* of the song *La bonne aventure, ô gué!* is an archaic form of *gai*, meaning 'gay'.

Stop instead at les Roches-l'Évêque, the first village so far with a good number of cave-houses, hollowed out from the 'tufa' cliff which here hems in the valley. It even has a cave-chapel, St Gervais, decorated with twelfth- and thirteenth-century frescoes.

Frescoes are a feature of many of the churches of this attractive valley. Some of the best, most of them of the twelfth century, are in the Chapel of St-Gilles at the little market town of Montoire three miles further on. Christ as the Pantocrator, the all-powerful, and as the Judge on the Last Day, here both dramatically executed, were among the favourite subjects of Romanesque artists everywhere in Europe.

St-Gilles is hidden, along with two other disused churches, in a corner of the older quarter on the left bank. The modern town of Montoire has grown up on the right bank, where its small railway station is. On its generally empty platform, looking north away from the town to countryside as French as one can find, took place on October 24th 1940 an historic interview between Adolf Hitler and the aged Marshal Pétain.

On a recent anniversary of Pétain's First World War victory at Verdun it was good to hear President Giscard d'Estaing – who in 1940 had barely entered his teens – pay the first official tribute since the war to this leader who perhaps saved France from a fate worse than that of Poland.

As at Vendôme, a ruined château stands above the left bank, whose steepness was better suited to the original fortification. An even more striking example of the same tendency stands a mile and a half up-river at Lavardin. Again, the castle is in ruins, which have had time to crumble magnificently since it was dismantled on the

orders of Henri IV nearly four hundred years ago. Not even Corfe
Castle or Bonaguil equal the effect of that jagged keep against the
skyline, with the remains of three lines of fortifications lying around
it. These allowed this Capetian outpost to resist two Plantagenet
sieges, one of which, in 1180, was directed by Henry II and Richard
Coeur de Lion in person.

The point from which to get the most impressive view of these
ruins is just above the church of St-Genest. Built on the hillside in
a very primitive Romanesque style in the eleventh century, this by
itself is sufficient excuse for visiting Lavardin. It contains remarkable frescoes executed over the four hundred years from the twelfth
century onwards.

The church of Lavardin is in competition not only with its own
castle, but with the more homogeneous murals of St-Jacques-des-
Guérets four miles downstream. Here thirteen paintings, each
framed by geometrically patterned borders, all belong to the same
twelfth century as the chapel itself. It lies on the same side of the
river as Lavardin, but is more easily reached by the right bank
across the bridge at Troo.

Troo is as odd as its name. At first sight a tiny fortified town with
a couple of gateways still standing, and dominated by a fine Angevin-
style church, it reveals itself on closer exploration as the cave capital
of France. One would have to go all the way to Guadix in Andalusia
to find as many troglodyte dwellings together, or a higher proportion of inhabitants living in them. Tufa façades, and gardens filled
with vegetables and flowers, add to the unreality of the walk along
narrow white footpaths, running parallel along the hillside, which
provide access to the 'front gates'.

Such a garden on the hillside at Troo, tended by an elderly man
in patched trousers, wearing a cloth cap rather than a beret, with
the Loir flowing quietly below, can seem the symbol of the whole
region, even more than the palatial châteaux.

But on the Loire itself, those châteaux and their memories are so
omnipresent that it is difficult to forget them, and to see through
the aristocratic tradition they represent to the more enduring
peasant reality beneath. Beside the less majestic Loir this is easier.

Yet the Loir inspired an even more aristocratic tradition, sur-
passing even that of Blois in the time of Charles d'Orléans, or Liré
in the youth of Joachim du Bellay. The source of this inspiration
lies only six miles down the valley, at the foot of the *coteaux* which

have here moved back some distance from the south bank. Here, in the simple but elegant *manoir* of La Possonière, was born on September 11th 1525 Pierre de Ronsard, perhaps the greatest court poet who ever lived. Even his earliest poems were closely modelled on the *Odes* of Pindar, the Greek poet who celebrated so exclusively the joys of aristocratic sport. He must be forgiven such artificiality, for what else could be expected when the outside walls of this early Renaissance house, built by his father, were embellished with sententious Latin inscriptions such as 'Truth, daughter of Time'?

With maturity, however, deeper feelings came to the surface, frequently for this countryside where he had grown up, where at Blois and Talcy he had known his first love, and at St Cosme where he was to die. As his stays at court lengthened from months into years his homesickness increased.

> *Quand je suis vingt ou trente mois*
> *Sans retourner en Vendômois,*
> *Plein de pensées vagabondes,*
> *Plein d'un remors et d'un souci,*
> *Aux rochers je me plains ainsi,*
> *Aux bois, aux antres et aux ondes.*

It was directed more particularly towards the river which ran almost at the bottom of his garden. To it he dedicated an *Ode à la source du Loir*.

> *Source d'argent toute pleine . . .*
> *De mon pays paternel . . .*
> *Sois tout orgueilleuse et fière*
> *De le baigner dans ton eau.*
> *Nulle française rivière*
> *N'en peut laver de plus beau.*

For despite those Latin inscriptions, La Possonière is far removed from Chambord or Cheverny, or even Chenonceaux, palaces imposed upon, rather than growing out of the countryside they dominate. Here for a moment the aristocratic tradition merges with that of the soil. The laureate of Catherine de Médicis identifies himself in stone in the decoration of his château with the *ronces ardentes*, blackberries, which echo his name. And his poem *A la forêt de Gastine* (the forest of Gâtine, which in part still survives) is more personal in feeling than *Woodman stay thy hand*, despite its classical imagery.

. . . Escoute, bucheron, (arreste un peu le bras);
Ce ne sont pas des bois que tu jettes à bas,
Ne vois-tu pas le sang, lequel degoute à force,
DesNymphes qui vivoient dessous la dure escorce?
Sacrilege, meurdrier, si on pend un voleur,
Pour piller un butin de bien peu de valeur,
Combien de feux, de fers, de morts, et de destresses
Merites-tu, meschant, pour tuer nos Deesses?
Forest, haute maison des oyseaux bocagers!
Plus le cerf solitaire et les chevreuls legers
Ne paistront sous ton ombre, et ta verte criniere
Plus du soleil d'esté ne rompra la lumiere.

This reconciliation of the traditions is only temporary. Just across the Loir is Poncé, with a Renaissance château far more different from the local building traditions. And thirteen miles downstream from Château-du-Loir (visited on the way from Le Mans to Tours) lies Le Lude, with a château cut off as dramatically by its deep, dried-up moats as by its architecture from the small town around it.

Its four massive corner towers do not hide its essentially residential character, partly because of the cheerful, unwarlike cream-coloured stone, and also because their crenellations and painted roofs belong more to some Ruritanian stage décor. The façades between them, one fifteenth-century Gothic, one François I Renaissance, and one Classical, might have been designed as a choice of sets for some gigantic opera.

Sets are just what they are each summer, when the château acts as the background to the biggest and most impressive of all the region's *Son et Lumière* spectacles. Three hundred and thirty figures in costume, some of them on horseback, some in carriages, and some even in barges, are added to the more usual voices and lighting to illustrate five centuries of history. The terraced gardens and the Loir itself beneath them add to the effect. Daytime visitors will also enjoy the interior of the château, which contains furniture, tapestries, and a fine collection of silk-embroidered court clothes of the eighteenth century.

To follow the Loir would lead in a few miles to La Flèche, which will be part of the next approach. So instead cut a corner by bearing off across country through pine-planted *gâtine* to the market town of Baugé. From a square in the centre there abruptly rises a simple château, with a single, narrow pepper-pot tower set in the side like a handle. It was built by Yolande of Aragon, mother of Le roi René, whose duchy of Anjou it is just inside.

The hospital of Baugé was built three centuries later, and is famous for its panelled pharmacy, filled with porcelain pots of the period. But older, and far more precious, is the True Cross of Baugé in the Chapel of the Incurables, brought back from Constantinople in the thirteenth century, and later decorated with gold and jewels. Its symbolic value is greater still. It was first adopted as a badge by the Dukes of Anjou. One of the many titles of Le roi René was also that of Duke of Lorraine, and so this 'double' cross became *La Croix de Lorraine*, chosen by General de Gaulle as the device of Free France.

Just outside the town, on the way to le Vieil-Baugé, which has an interesting church, took place in 1421 a battle which cost the life of Henry V's brother Clarence. But the present route runs due west, along the last section of the useful road already crossed at Neuillé-Pont-Pierre, which runs all the way from Blois to Seiches. Seiches is a large village where the Loir, whenever I cross it there, seems everything that a peaceful, reflective *rivière* should be.

But it is near its end. The main road from Le Mans, which joins the route at Seiches, takes a short cut to Angers. In those twelve miles the Loir has merged with the Sarthe, and the combined stream has almost immediately emptied itself into the Mayenne. Mayenne, the name of this river and of a town on its banks, and Maine, the name of the province and of the river formed by Mayenne, Sarthe and Loir together, are in origin the same ancient, probably even pre-Celtic word.

There are two sides to the character of the *département* of Maine-et-Loire, and of the preceding province of Anjou, of which it is and was the capital. An historian of mediaeval England, who had perhaps never himself been there, described the Plantagenets' home county as a land of gaiety, laughter and wine, where spring was not only earlier, but infinitely more intoxicating than in England. But the novelist Peter de Polnay, on the other hand, who perhaps knows the land all too well, has conveyed in *Death of a Patriot* the featureless monotony of some of the Angevin villages, with their one-storeyed grey houses lining a long, wide road.

These two views are not necessarily in direct opposition. Suggestions of both will occur to anyone exploring the region around where the three *rivières* meet, as you will in order to reach two important châteaux with confusingly similar names: Le Plessis-Bourré and Le Plessis-Macé. The word *plessis* comes from the Latin *plexum*, meaning an enclosed space.

Le Plessis-Bourré stands alone, gleaming white behind its huge moat on the plain between Sarthe and Mayenne. Jean Bourré, Louis XI's treasurer, started to build it in 1468 after he had finished Langeais. Like this, it is a comfortable house as well as a defensible *château-fort*, not only in its moat, but in its general construction. Until 1488 Brittany was still a powerful independent state, and while Langeais blocked the route up the Loire from Nantes, this castle is almost on the Breton frontier.

The climax of the tour round the beautifully furnished interior is the panelled ceiling of the guardroom. Each panel is painted with a fifteenth-century scene representing some popular proverb, with a Chaucerian or even Rabelaisian sense of humour.

Le Plessis-Macé, at the heart of a village of the same name, just to the left of the main road from Angers to Rennes, was even nearer the former frontier, and its outer walls, defended by a now dry moat, and crowned by four round towers, date from as early as the twelfth century. The ruined keep, and the Flamboyant chapel with its carved screen, date from the fifteenth.

Fourteen miles farther along the same road is Segré. It has no specific monument worth attention, but more than a fair share of Angevin *ambiance* around its bridges over, and roads alongside, the little river Oudon. It is another fifteen miles to Pouancé, squeezed between two lakes on the frontier itself. Its shabby but impressive château, with nine round towers, stands beside one of them.

And so back to Angers. Although not technically on the Loire, it is very much a city of the Loire Valley. The Maine in its brief course of five miles simply widens a valley already broadened by the Authion, a curious stream which runs parallel to the Loire at a distance of from two to five miles all the way from near Bourgueil.

It is an unexpectedly big city. Its 140,000 odd inhabitants make it third only to Tours and Nantes along the river, and third to Tours and Le Mans in the region. It was a large place even in the days when it served as the capital of the Plantagenets, or of Le roi René.

As so often in France, the mediaeval walls which enclosed it on both sides of the Maine have been replaced by a series of boule-vards. The opportunity was taken to put aside a vast open space just

beyond these. Half is a pleasant public garden, and half a weekly
market with a car park, where you would do well to leave any
vehicle before venturing into the older part of the town. Or you can
start with the most important of all the monuments of Angers.

This, the château, occupying an immense corner between a
boulevard and the Maine, has ample parking space near the main
gate, which leads through its gloomy patterned flint outer walls,
with their seventeen decapitated towers. Inside the atmosphere is
lighter. Much of the area is formal gardens, such as Le roi René
himself loved, while those buildings which remain were for the
most part erected either by him or by his father. They include an
exquisite Flamboyant chapel (in which a stained-glass window
shows Le roi René and his queen), with the adjacent Royal lodgings
and Châtelet, and the Governor's lodgings attached directly to a
distant corner of the ramparts.

All these buildings now contain exhibits from the *Musée des
Tapisseries*. This is the richest of its kind in the world, and many
of them, such as the Lady at the Organ in the Governor's lodgings,
would by themselves make the château famous. But it possesses a
greater tapestry still – or rather a whole series of tapestries. A special
gallery was built twenty-five years ago to house it.

The *Tenture de L'Apocalypse* widens appreciation of the mediaeval world on several different levels. Its sheer size – originally
some 550 feet long by 18 feet high – tells much about the scale of
princely living when it was ordered in 1373 by René's grandfather,
Louis I of Anjou. Its near-loss at the Revolution, and again when
the cathedral, which had inherited it, twice put it up for sale, shows
how much has been lost from that age. The fact that it accompanied
the Dukes on their journeys to their other châteaux in Anjou,
Lorraine or Provence shows how nomadic was aristocratic life, even
as late as the fifteenth century. Finally the scenes themselves,
worked on red and blue backgrounds following fairly closely the
text of Revelations – St John the Divine appears as an observer on
the left of every picture – portray, especially in their incidentals, the
life of the time when they were woven in Paris by Nicolas Bataille.
He was paid the unheard-of sum of 6,000 livres: today perhaps
£100,000.

A walk along the ramparts of the château gives a clear idea of the
layout of the town astride the Maine, and in particular of the suburb
of la Doutre beyond the river. There stood several of the religious

foundations which before the Revolution dominated the life of Angers with their petty rivalries (these have been brilliantly studied and described by Professor McManners). Three buildings survive: the twelfth-century church of la Trinité, the even earlier Romanesque abbey-church of the Ronceray nearby, and the hospital of St-Jean.

This was started in 1180 when Henry II still ruled here, and completed in 1210 when Philip II had taken the Loire Valley from his son. It is one of the finest examples of the 'Angevin' style which was successfully transplanted to the Plantagenet kingdom across the Channel and there known as Early English. It is especially evident in the vaulted roof of the *grande salle*, a vast hall which now holds an updated version of the *Tenture de l'Apocalypse*. Called the Chant du Monde, this is a Gobelins designed by that master of the French tapestry revival, Jean Lurçat. Other parts of the ancient hospital open to visit are the cloister, the chapel, and the former storehouse, called the Greniers St-Jean, which contains a wine museum in its cellars.

Back across the Maine, in the central part of the town, there are further examples of Angevin architecture in the church of St-Serge, and in the nave of the cathedral, which has stained-glass windows of the same period. Choir and transepts are Gothic. The Préfecture was another former abbey. There are also many fine old private houses, such as the fifteenth-century Maison d'Adam. Two such houses, the Renaissance Logis Pincé, and the Logis Barrault of 1487, are now museums.

The industries which have caused the modern growth of Angers range from umbrellas to computers. The most noticeable are that of the seed merchants, whose flower beds brighten much of the surrounding district, and the less colourful slate which roofs many of the city's buildings. The slate quarries are centred on Trélazé, four miles out on the plain between Maine and Loire, beyond the gleaming new *zone industrielle* which contains the most interesting of all the factories of Angers.

The word 'Cointreau' has for so long represented to me a piquant sweetness and a feeling of controlled well-being despite repletion, that it came as a surprise to learn that it was simply that of a family. The liqueur 'born of the happy marriage between the alcohol of Angers and oranges ripened under the sun of the Tropics' was first produced in 1849 by the two brothers Édouard and Adolphe

Cointreau on the site in the city centre where the distillery remained until it moved to the *zone industrielle* in 1971. Today it is still under the direct management of their descendants: the brothers Robert and Max Cointreau, and their cousin Pierre. Their name is in fact highly suitable for the drink they export to 217 markets. Ultimately derived from the same root as the English a*cquaint*ance, it is an Angevin diminutive of *coint*, an archaic word meaning elegant.

The family is prominent in the public as well as the commercial life of the region. Robert Cointreau, for example, is *Grand Commandeur* of the *Chevaliers de Sacavin*. He recently welcomed a delegation of the English branch of this brotherhood to a gathering in Fontevrault abbey. The previous evening they had been entertained by the local *Association Franco-Britannique*, the 'Club des Plantagenêts d'Angers'. A new cocktail was launched for the occasion. It consisted of one part of Cointreau, three of Saumur sparkling wine, and a dash of the yellow Izarra liqueur from the Basque country. It was christened 'Le Plantagenêt'.

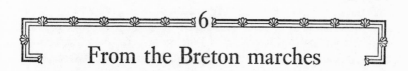

6

From the Breton marches

The first impressions of most Britons visiting France for the first time, as they drive south and west from the Channel ports, are of greater distances, fewer people and straighter roads than they expected. An impression, too, of towns and provinces until now only dimly heard of – Pas-de-Calais, Picardie, Pontoise – making them wonder if they have forgotten all their geography, or failed to do their homework before setting out.

This impression is perhaps even stronger for those disembarking from the new ferries to Cherbourg, St Malo or Roscoff, and heading south and east through Fougères. Brittany and Normandy have at least been familiar names, as have the landing beaches and battlefields of the last War. But when the '35' car registration number of Ille-et-Vilaine (often seen together with the 'Bzh' nationalist plaque displayed by many Bretons, even those who have no desire for devolution), is replaced by '53', or when a notice announces 'Mayenne', many travellers enter something of a mental limbo.

What is this unknown, backwoods *département* of Mayenne, or the unsuspected province of Maine referred to in the local tourist notices and brochures, or the chic little city of Laval, mysteriously appearing where a valley interrupts the ruler-straight road?

And straight it is, the Fougères to Tours road, once it has entered the region and shaken off the twists and turns of a Celtic highway, but it is only straight in one plane. In the other it is a long series of steep ups and downs – fun to drive along only because there is so little traffic.

A few miles after leaving Brittany a notice points to the abbey of Clermont down a road to the right. Founded by St Bernard himself in the mid-twelfth century, it is today a monument one pays to visit like any other. But in the 50s and 60s it was the home of a vague lay order, restricted apparently neither by sex nor doctrine. It was a slightly eerie experience to be conducted round the magnificent white interior of the remote Cistercian church by a retired lady or a friendly youth, breathing sentiments of pleasant but diffuse philanthropy far removed from the stern ideals of Clairvaux.

A monastery where even sterner ideals are still practised lies some twelve miles away, and can be reached across country without passing through Laval. The abbey of Port-Salut belongs to the modern successors of the Cistercians, the Trappists, and has less architectural interest. But its site beside the peaceful river Mayenne is enchanting. The efficient factory where they make the famous cheese can be visited at certain hours. The process was learned by the monks when in exile in Westphalia during the Revolution.

Either of these abbeys would serve as good starting points for a tour of the southern part of the department of Mayenne. Its two centres are Château-Gontier on the river, and Craon, known for its breed of pigs (*les blancs de l'Ouest*), and for its Louis XVI château with formal gardens.

Six miles south of Craon, off the road to Segré, the very different château of Mortier-Crolles behind its moat belongs to the very end of the fifteenth century. In a pleasing pattern of brick and tufa – dull red and old gold – it is one of the most important examples in the region of the transformation of the mediaeval *château-fort* into a Renaissance residence.

The most abiding impression of this rather uniform countryside confirms the name of 'le Maine noir' by which it is often known; it is an extension to the north of the Segréen or 'Anjou noir'; and both owe the *noir* to their dark slate roofs. However there is nothing dull or gloomy about the banks of the Mayenne, which contribute greatly to the attraction of Laval. The twelfth-century round keep of the Vieux-Château and a number of old houses make with a thirteenth-century bridge a fine riverscape. A visit to the museums housed in the châteaux enables one to enjoy the Renaissance additions as well. One of these museums is devoted to *Art Naïf*, since it was at Laval that that greatest of primitives, the *douanier* Rousseau, was born.

The nearby cathedral (which was only given that status in 1855) is less interesting than the Romanesque Notre-Dame d'Avénières on the other bank. More interesting still is the smaller and older pre-Romanesque church of Notre-Dame de Pritz, the original parish church of the town, a couple of miles upstream. The thirteenth-century frescoes include a calendar with pictures of each month's agricultural tasks.

The smart shops and lively air of this town of 50,000 inhabitants are due to its being not only the capital of the *département* of Mayenne, but also one of the rare industrial centres of the West. Its most important product, textiles, dates from as long ago as 1289, when the bride of a Count of Laval brought along weavers from her native Flanders.

The town, twenty miles to the north, which actually bears the name Mayenne, is only a quarter the size. It is suitably dependent for its attraction on the river to which it slopes steeply down. There are quays along the banks, and more views of it from the walk along the walls of the remains of the castle.

The Dukes of Mayenne were important figures. One, the younger brother of the two Guises murdered at Blois, led the Catholic armies against Henri IV. The former ducal law court, with two sundials on the façade, stands at the top of the main street.

Although Mayenne is on the main Route Nationale 12 from Paris to Brittany, there are places of great interest near it which are seldom visited. Ten miles north the perfectly preserved and still lived-in château of Lassay shows, with its eight towers in weathered granite, what a mid-fifteenth-century castle really looked like. A mile away to the north-west of Lassay the ruined châteaux of le Bois-Thibault and le Bois-Froult, set against a wooded background, evoke the past even more. Another fifteenth-century château set in a forest is

Bourgon, off a byroad six miles south-east of Mayenne. But the most important monument in this direction is far older.

The Roman fortress at Jublains, just outside the village on the road to Montsûrs, is an uneven square measuring nearly four hundred feet on each side. Its massive stone outer walls still stand fifteen feet high and broad. It is commonly described simply as a fortified post protecting the routes to Armorica (Brittany). But there was evidently a small town covering a far larger area under the early empire. It seems likely that this impressive third-century building became the home of the survivors of the barbarian attacks of the years between 250 and 275.

Once you are so far out of your way as Mayenne and Jublains, there is an opportunity of rejoining the main road to Tours by a far more interesting route than the straight road from Laval through Meslay-du-Maine, though I have happy memories of nights spent at the inn there. The road is so monotonous, with dull one-storeyed nineteenth-century cottages in the rare hamlets, that for years I drove swiftly through them without ever suspecting that there were excitements only a few miles to the east.

First after Jublains comes the Château du Rocher, just outside the village of Mézangers. It is a mixture of late mediaeval and Renaissance, with the latter contributing a beautiful open gallery.

Another three miles, with the Coëvron hills already met on the 'Maine road' looming like dark mountains on the left, take you to the small town of Evron. Its church combines a Romanesque nave with a much larger Gothic choir. The adjoining twelfth-century chapel of Notre-Dame de l'Épine, entered when I was there only by a long walk round narrow lanes, has much restored frescoes, and the thirteenth-century statue and other treasures of this patroness of Evron. Beside the church stands the abbey which once it served. This huge Louis XV building now houses a women's religious order. It is best appreciated by passing through the gateway from the square in front of the church. A walk beside the long façade enables one to look down on the sheltered sunken gardens, which are in some ways its most monastic part.

Four miles along the same road stands the smaller but even more interesting town of Ste-Suzanne, still surrounded by the later mediaeval walls replacing those which had defied William the Conqueror. Small signs direct the visitor round, and point out such monuments as the Porte de Fer and the Tour Sud. The eleventh-

century keep, and the château built in 1608 by Fouquet de la
Varenne, who first started a public postal service in France, require
a ticket for a prolonged visit, but a good general impression can be
taken in free from the entrance. The best part of the walk round the
ramparts is the Promenade de la Poterne above the little river Ervé.
It looks across to the last heights of the string of hills reaching from
the Mont des Avaloirs. Here they are covered by the wide forest of
La Grande Charnie.

The road to follow from Ste-Suzanne is the one which keeps
closest to the Ervé. The next place of interest, nine miles on, is
directly beside the river, or rather, on both sides: to the left the
Grotte à Margot (named after a witch who is said to have hidden
treasure there); and to the right the Grotte Rochefort.

However the real attraction of the Grottes de Saulges is not their
stalactites and stalagmites, and not even the prehistoric paintings of
a third cave, which are still under seal, but their position. The cliffs
in which they lie surround a perfect green basin, with the Ervé
running beside an ancient mill, and a functional modern restaurant
providing delicious but expensive meals. I camped there for three
days, watching a nephew fishing in the Ervé with newly made
French friends, and climbing up to the plateau to buy supplies at
the village of Saulges; these are my happiest memories of this
corner of Lower Maine.

The village has both a Gothic parish church and a smaller, pre-
Romanesque, Carolingian church. The return journey to the caves
may be made along the right bank of the river, passing the sixteenth-
century chapel of St Cénéré. This was the brother of that other
hermit St Céneri, whose sanctuary is forty miles north in the Alpes
Mancelles.

Rejoining the N 159, you quickly come into Upper Maine –
since 1791 the Sarthe – and then almost at once into Sablé, through
which flows the river that gave its name to the modern *département*.
Although it has always had a certain importance – the Dukes of
Brittany signed a humiliating peace here in 1488 – it leaves little
impression on the passing motorist, seeming as colourless as its
'sandy' name.

Yet with closer acquaintance local detail stands out. Sablé's
maire, M. le Theule, is an active campaigner for rural revival, not
only in his own town, but throughout the *département*. He has done
for Sarthe what M. Pisani has achieved for Maine-et-Loire, and

M. Buron for Mayenne. The old people's home in the converted château of La Martinière is a model of its kind. And when at last one evening, travelling north, I turned right for Solesmes, I wondered why I had not lingered longer and earlier beside this rewarding *rivière*.

A couple of miles upstream the opposite left bank rises slightly, and the elevation of the land is continued by a stone structure dropping sheer to the river. The first impression is of a fortress, the second, on seeing the large number of windows on the grim façade, is of a Tibetan monastry. The second impression is nearer the truth.

Until it was closed at the Revolution, Solesmes was a relatively unimportant priory, but it was chosen in 1833 by Dom Guéranger, a native of Sablé, as his starting point for the revival of the Benedictine Order in France. During the century which followed it not only grew out of the eighteenth-century buildings of the priory into the impressive neo-Gothic mass seen from across the Sarthe, but also spread the order across France and even further afield. Farnborough and Quarr in England are both its foundations.

Solesmes has done more than grow: on the deepest spiritual level it has become the heart of Catholicism in *l'Ouest*, and on an intellectual level it has from its earliest days attracted writers anxious to *se recueillir*, which is under-translated by 'go into retreat'. Lacordaire was here as early as 1838, and later St Exupéry and Simone Weil. In France as a whole it holds a special place in the development of the religious arts.

The first of these is music. Gregorian plainsong can here be enjoyed in all its clear beauty. I always arrange my own visits to Solesmes to coincide either with the daily High Mass at quarter to ten in the morning, or the Vespers at five in the afternoon. The whole or the original abbey church has become a long nave, from which the public watches the black or white figures in the newer choir beyond the *clôture*. Nor are the other listeners without interest: the tense youth a few seats ahead may prove to be the St Exupéry of the 1990s. On my last visit I noticed an unusually large number of younger people, in flared jeans and fur anoraks (go warmly clothed if the weather is anything less than hot, for the nave seems to distil all the cold and damp of *l'Ouest*). They turned out to be the final year from the *Conservatoire* of Lausanne, who had specially requested a course on the interpretation of mediaeval music which only certain of the Solesmes fathers were qualified to give.

Another art cherished here is sculpture. Dom Guéranger himself finished off the sixteenth-century wooden stalls of the choir, and the statue on his own tomb is an interesting work of between the two wars. There is inspiration to hand in the Saints of Solesmes, a set of sculpted groups in the two arms of the transept. The village would still be famous for these if the monks never returned.

The *Burial of Christ*, to the right, dating from 1496, is clearly by a master, possibly the great Michel Colomb, though more recently experts have preferred the almost unknown 'un certain Lambert ou Larembert'. But the combination of Flamboyant details in most of the figures with the 'Classical' equipment of the two brutal-looking soldiers is typical of the later Colomb, just at the transition of Gothic to Renaissance. The faces of Joseph of Arimathaea and of Nicodemus must surely have been taken from living old men. St Mary Magdalene meditates sadly alone in the foreground. The other groups, to the left, belong to half a century later. They deal with aspects of the life of Our Lady: her last Communion, her burial, her Assumption, her Triumph. Here the details are uncompromisingly Renaissance.

Similar scenes, but in a different medium and earlier, from the twelfth to the fourteenth centuries, can be found in the frescoes of the Romanesque church of Asnières-sur-Vègre, five miles further east. Nearby the château of Verdelles stands just as it was built – no alterations, no additions – about the same time that the *Burial of Christ* was being carved at Solesmes.

Having thus left the Sarthe to go a couple of miles up its small tributary, the Vègre, it would be a pity not to continue another ten miles to Loué. On the way the ruins of the castle of L'Isle stand in a loop of the stream. Loué has no particular monument. But it was chosen by François Reichenbach as the setting for a film about that idealised life in the country that so many urban Frenchmen dream of. Since then it has featured in a number of nostalgic magazine articles on the life by the *rivières* of the *Pays de la Loire*.

Back on the N 159, dead straight for fourteen miles after Sablé, you soon reach La Flèche, the biggest town between Laval and Tours. The restful Loir is here particularly pleasing, dammed between two old mills to form a lake beside which the fifteenth-century château has been adapted as the town hall. A bridge across a branch of the river gives access to one of the best situated camp sites of the region, adding a touch of blue and orange colour across the water to the main road through the town. On a sunny day it is hard to agree with Gresset's deadly condemnation of 1729:

> *Un climat assez agreable,*
> *De petits bois assez mignons,*
> *Un petit vin assez potable,*
> *De petits concerts assez bons,*
> *Un petit monde assez passable,*
> *La Flèche pourrait être aimable*
> *S'il était de belles prisons.*

Its centre – *Sous-préfecture*, post office, thirteenth-century church of St Thomas – lies off the road to the left. The institution for which La Flèche is famous lies further behind again.

Le Prytanée was founded in 1604 by Henri IV, when he presented the Jesuits with a house he had inherited from his parents. (They had been staying in it nine months before his birth, so that he was conceived here, and could be described as 'Fléchois before having been Béarnais'.) One of the Jesuits' pupils was Descartes. But on their expulsion in 1762, the college was used to prepare officers for the army of Louis XV, and was reestablished on still more military lines by Napoleon. From the seven companies under the command of captains into which its 1,200 pupils are divided have come eleven Marshals of France.

The entry gate with the valuable library above is of the mid-seventeenth century. Most of the rest was built over a century later, but the oldest and most interesting part of the Prytanée is its early seventeenth-century chapel. Its white interior, with angels bearing the instruments of the Passion, is a Baroque extravaganza which would have delighted Marie de Médicis, whose heart lies here with that of her husband Henri IV. They were burned during the Revolution, and their ashes now share a single casket.

Passing through Le Lude, visited on the way along the Loir to Angers, another twenty-three miles brings you to Château-la-Vallière – an evocative name, though this upland township, set in poor, forested *gâtine*, is hardly the background one would have imagined for the young Louis XIV's best loved mistress Louise. He created her Duchess of La Vallière, and she founded an alms-house here, which still owns a portrait of her in the robes of the

Carmelite Order she entered when her term as favourite was over. The pleasantest view of the place is from the far side of the lake to the south.

Two personal experiences here show how far it is not only from the court of the Sun King, but from modern Tours only twenty miles away. One is of a service in the parish church, where my neighbour was a tiny, birdlike widow. Her black costume, of some timeless cut, could have belonged as easily to 1923 as to 1973. The other is of my visit to the ruined mediaeval château of Vaujours, two miles away in the adjacent forest. I stopped to chat to a cultured woman of perhaps seventy, living on her pension in a cottage surrounded by a well-filled *potager*. In her patched but clean dress, in her cultivation of most of her own food, and in her contempt for television but love of the radio, she summed up much of the best of the plain, basic values of this whole region.

From this world, and from the lightly-populated, wooded *gâtine* which continues all the way back to the road from Le Mans, the transition is abrupt as you once again drop down the steep hill, cross the eighteenth-century bridge, and drive at once into the heart of Tours. On the left a large modern building with huge windows stands over the Loire. It is the Municipal Library, a rare thing in this literary land so short of readers, but appropriate in the presence of Rabelais and Descartes, whose statues are on the left and right of the road running along the quays.

You are now in the rue Nationale – before the Revolution the rue Royale – lined by choice specialist shops and department stores. On it, or within easy reach of it, there also lie all the older buildings of the original city, which lay immediately south of the river. The continuation of the rue Nationale called the avénue de Grammont, lined by useful but rather less elegant shops, leads in a couple of miles to the Cher, the important tributary which for many miles runs parallel and close to the Loire. The place Jean-Jaurès marks where the *rue* ends and the *avenue* begins. Here they are crossed at right angles by the series of boulevards which mark the limits reached by the city about 1600. In a ponderous line stand the post office, the Palais de Justice, and the Hôtel de Ville, the office of M Royer, Mayor of Tours, candidate at the 1974 presidential elections, and a well-publicised campaigner on the place of hypermarkets and of prostitution, in both Tours and generally.

A few yards left (west), in the square opposite the railway

station, a plate-glass *Syndicat d'Initiative* is staffed by smartly uniformed hostesses whose good looks but somewhat off-putting sophistication might serve as a symbol for the city they serve. They have an excuse, in this capital of the *châteaux de la Loire*, for their *blasé* attitude, as the hundredth scruffy youth asks for the cheapest hotel room in Tours, or the twentieth American demands where he can catch a bus to Loches. She will tell the latter 'just outside', for the *Gare Routière* in the square is also a halt for the long-distance coaches from Paris to all parts of the Iberian peninsula. There is something out of place about the peasant faces of immigrant workers lining the windows of the coaches from Oviedo or Oporto. But I have found these services very useful myself, and Tours a convenient centre to embark from or to meet people on their way to and from Spain.

The railway station is far less international in character. The main line to Bordeaux and Madrid only skirts the city. From the junction in the industrial suburb of St-Pierre-des-Corps a *navette* or link train runs backwards and forwards on the small branch line to the Gare de Tours.

Further exploration of the city should be done on foot, with the car parked, ideally, somewhere along the quays, with the view across the Loire to return to.

Large areas of the old city on both sides of the rue Nationale were burned out during the German attack between June 18th and 20th 1940. As a result the two centres of Tours, the original Roman city around the cathedral, and the quarter which grew up around the tomb of St Martin, right outside the walls to the west, are once again separated, though now by tall, dull modern buildings instead of fields.

The one ancient building which survived this destruction is the thirteenth-century abbey church of St Julien. It gives almost straight on to the rue Nationale only a short distance from the Loire. The bombardment caused considerable damage, and repairs are particularly noticeable in the bell tower above the entrance. This is the only surviving part of a Romanesque church three hundred years older.

The church stands well below the present road level, as do the adjacent buildings belonging to the former abbey. These include the twelfth-century chapter house, where Henri III called the Parlement de Paris in 1589; cellars with a museum of the history and present production of the wines of Touraine; and on the floor above the one and only *Musée du Compagnonnage*.

The *compagnons* to whose work and way of life this is dedicated stand somewhere between the original Freemasons who built the mediaeval cathedrals, and modern trade unionists. When the mediaeval guilds were becoming employers' federations, of which the livery companies of the City of London are descendants, these trained artisans banded together to defend their conditions and salaries, and also their standards of workmanship.

Such activity was frowned on long before Tolpuddle. It had to be carried on in secret, with ceremonial initiation rites and an organised underground network. But the most fascinating point is that the *compagnons* have emerged into the open, and into the industrial world of today, with the two most important features of their training still intact.

The first is that the young man who has completed his apprenticeship – the 'journeyman', in fact, as he was once known in England – must still set off on his *tour de France*. In each town where he arrives for a few months he can rely upon the help of full *compagnons* established there. They will find him work and lodging, or perhaps put him up themselves. Often the *Compagnonnage* itself will own a house there where he can have a room. The experience gained in a year or two of such travelling is fully comparable with the mind-broadening (as opposed to the purely academic) effect of going to a university. I always feel respect when a voice on the radio, or a hitch-hiker I have picked up, tells me in a confident though unpretentious tone that he has made, or is making, his *tour de France*.

The second important survival is that he must prove himself fit for initiation by showing his skills in a *chef d'oeuvre* or masterpiece. Here in the Museum is an extraordinary selection of these by candidates for a wide variety of trades. One leaves not only with wonder at human ingenuity, but with confidence in the wholesomeness of an important part of French society.

The fires of 1940 destroyed less to the west of the rue Nationale than to the east. The narrow streets just behind St-Julien still contain many houses from the fifteenth and sixteenth centuries, when Tours was frequently the royal residence. The rue Colbert, once the main street of the city, and the picturesque rue de la Scellerie, are both worth following. Both lead towards the Cathedral of

St-Gatien, whose twin towers are like those of many Renaissance
churches in Spain, and can be seen across the roofs from much
further away. In my mind's eye they are still visible, without intervening buildings, from beyond the Loire, as they were when first I
gazed on the still-ravaged Tours of 1948. When their sculpture and
design are examined in closer detail it will be seen that they are not
quite alike. The south tower was completed forty years after the
north had been finished in 1507.

1547 is the date when the façade too was finished, after 337 years
of continuous building. *'Interminable comme l'oeuvre de St Maurice'* is
still a *tourangeau* saying – the cathedral was originally dedicated to
him. This long construction makes it a living memorial of the
development of Gothic, Flamboyant, and finally the Renaissance,
of which it has the overall look from a distance. The earliest of these
periods produced the fifteen magnificent stained-glass windows of
the choir. *Genesis* (fourth from the left) and the *Legend of St Martin*
(tenth from the left) are particularly fine.

To the left of the Cathedral is the cloister of the Psallette. This
word means 'mastership in music', and the choir school was once
situated here. In the last century it was divided into apartments,
one of which Balzac wrote of as the home of the leading female
character of his *Curé de Tours*.

On the other side of the cathedral the former archbishops' palace now holds the *Musée des Beaux-Arts*. Its seventeenth- and
eighteenth-century construction has allowed the use of appropriate
woodwork, hangings and furniture, suitably to vary the décor of
each room to go with the pictures exhibited. The most famous of
these are two Mantegnas, *Christ in the Garden of Olives* and *The
Resurrection*.

It is not only the inside of the museum that has atmosphere. The
archbishops' garden is illuminated every summer evening until
mid-September, and filled between nine and eleven with classical
music from hidden loudspeakers. A stroll amongst the lawns and
shrubberies to the accompaniment of Vivaldi or Mozart is one of
the pleasantest cultural experiences of a *tourangeau* summer.

It need not be the only one. Concerts are given at the end of
June and beginning of July at the Grange de Meslay, five miles out
on the road to Paris. This vast tithe barn, belonging to a farm once
owned by the monks of Marmoutier, stands just as it was erected
about 1220. The roof timbers rest on four lines of supporting

pillars, all of chestnut wood. Quite exceptional acoustics combine with an unusual and venerable setting.

The concerts of Meslay are part of a festival which includes first-class theatre and other events in the place Plumereau. This square is the centre of the other older section of the town to have survived June 1940, away to the west of the rue Nationale. Surrounded by gabled half-timbered houses, it could equally well be in a market town of England or Germany. Elsewhere in this quarter, later influences are more obvious. The fifteenth- and sixteenth-century Hotel Gouin is a private palace now occupied by the Archaeological Museum. Here are the instruments used for experiments in physics by Jean-Jacques Rousseau during his stay at Chenonceaux.

The *Centre d'Études Supérieures de la Renaissance* in the rue Néricault-Destouches was founded by the late Pierre Mansard on the lines of the *Centre d'Etudes Supérieures de Civilisation Mediévale* at Poitiers. The location of these two *centres* was determined by the widespread Romanesque style of Poitu, and the Renaissance style of Touraine. The Renaissance *stages*, again in July, bring to Tours experts and research students from all over the world to share lectures and discussion on a different theme each year: Mannerism, perhaps, or the discovery of America.

More general education is given to far larger numbers of foreigners throughout the whole year at the nearby *Institut de Touraine*. This is one of the oldest established and best known centres for the study of French language and civilisation. My own impression from hearing the odd lecture is that it is leaning back rather too much on the prized *tourangeau* accent which is its greatest selling point. On the other hand I have yet to meet a student who has not enjoyed his or her stay there. They talk of the friendships made, the visits to châteaux, the fun of such local events as the Garlic Fair on July 26th, and the walks home on summer nights through the old streets.

During their history lectures they will have been encouraged to take the bus the two miles to Plessis-lès-Tours, the plain late fifteenth-century château where Louis XI spent his last twenty years planning to unite France. During their lectures in modern literature they will have been urged to walk across the Loire to see the houses where great writers found inspiration: Anatole France at *La Béchellerie*; Balzac at *La Grenadière*; Bergson at *La Gaudinière*. During their studies of Renaissance poetry they should, if they have any imagination, walk along the left bank to the beautifully restored priory of St Cosme. This is a sanctuary as sacred as that cemetery beside the pyramid of Caius Cestius which shelters the last remains of Keats and Shelley. For here, in the fifteenth-century house where he had often composed looking across the Loire, Pierre de Ronsard died two days after Christmas in 1585. Here too he is buried.

Among all these distractions, though, some may spare a thought for the greatest *tourangeau* of all, whose life made all that has followed possible, for they will often pass by the basilica of St Martin. This replaces an earlier building, larger than the cathedral, which during the Middle Ages had attracted one of the great pilgrimages of Christendom. Pulled down in 1802 to make way for the rue des Halles, this has left only the Tour de l'Horloge, the Tour Charlemagne, and its cloister to testify to its age and size.

The new basilica, a neo-Byzantine construction finished half a century ago, covers only a third of the area of the old, and with only half of that on the former site, but it does, vitally, include the saint's tomb. So this last approach has led to the first protagonist of the *juste milieu* which has ever since characterised Touraine, and to the true heart of the Loire Valley.

The

UNCLASPED NECKLACE

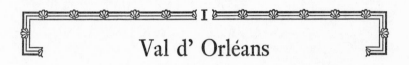

I

Val d' Orléans

Although you have touched the Loire at its three great cities of Orléans, Blois and Tours, so far you have only followed it from Gien upstream to Nevers. Now, aware of its countryside of *gâtine*, *rivières* and *bocage*, of the historical events to which it has been a background, and having approached it in every direction open to visitors from the north, it is time to go down the river itself. The journey is like examining one by one the pearls of an unclasped necklace: the succession of châteaux which are its greatest glory.

First of these after Gien is Sully-sur-Loire. High above the left bank behind a wide moat rises a dream of a mediaeval castle, complete with parapets, curtain wall, drawbridge, and towers crowned with those pepper-pot roofs which were the trademark of French mediaeval architecture. It is easy to imagine Joan of Arc riding out from here in 1430 on her last expedition, which was to lead to her capture. The building dates from 1363, and has great chestnut roof beams like those of the Grange de Meslay.

The body of the Duke of Sully, the great minister of Henri IV, lies in the chapel of this older fortress. The wing which he rebuilt, and where he spent his thirty-one years of retirement, is behind this. Here are his bedroom and study. Born Maximilien de Béthune, and known during the long campaigns from Gascony to Normandy as the Marquis de Rosny, he bought the castle in 1602. He was only created Duke of Sully four years before his career ended with his master's assassination in 1610. His descendants were neither so seriousminded, nor so loyal to the Bourbons, as the stern Protestant minister of finances. Voltaire, who came here when exiled under the Régence, knew that he could expect a permissive life style as well as political sympathy. Sully might not have approved of the

Nuits Galantes, which was written and first performed here, but he would have warmed to the young Voltaire working on the *Henriade*, the eighteenth century's tribute to his King's restoration of French prosperity.

Crossing to the right bank, almost immediately a minor road to the left along the top of the retaining *levée* provides a good opportunity for taking in the extent of the Valley at its widest stretch. Between Cosne and Orléans, where the sands of the Sologne offered little resistance, it often covers five miles. The immense skies of the Loire never seem vaster. The village which now appears ahead might well lie in the very centre of France.

That was the actual belief of the Gauls, who met in council every year on the site of St-Benoît-sur-Loire. It was here, in the seventh century, that the abbey of Fleury was founded, which acquired in 673 the body of St Benedict, and in due course his name, and became the greatest centre of learning of Charlemagne's Empire. Its situation just within the narrow royal domain of the early Capetians was one of the aces in their apparently weak hand.

To that early Capetian period belong the most striking parts of the present church. The massive porch has sixteen pillars whose flanking columns have fascinating carved capitals giving a view of the world of the early 1100s. The transept and the superb choir date from the later years of the same century. This overwhelming Romanesque character is hardly disturbed by the Transitional nave, and is reinforced by the large circular crypt. This is half a century earlier even than the porch. Here pilgrims could see and venerate the casket containing the relics of St Benedict.

This they can once again do today; since 1944 the abbey has again housed the Benedictines, and in the crypt one of them, after accompanying you round the building, will describe to you their present-day life. Whatever your language, there will almost certainly be a monk there who speaks it, for the Order retains its international flavour, and Fleury its intellectual distinction.

St-Benoît was where the poet Max Jacob, a friend of Picasso and his circle in Paris in the early years of the century, retired, and here beneath the great abbey at the heart of Gaul, he was converted to Catholicism, and later taken by the Gestapo to martyrdom in a concentration camp. A well set-out gallery on the ground floor of the *Musée des Beaux-Arts* at Orléans is devoted to his life and work.

Three miles on, and out of sight of the river, is Germigny-des-

Prés. Its small church behind a little garden was claimed by its *curé* on my own visit to be the oldest in France. In the sense of its being an original construction still in regular use, he is certainly right. It was built in 806 by Theodulf, bishop of Orléans and abbot of Fleury. He was one of the great figures in the entourage of Charlemagne, that ruler who for one brief moment in the Dark Ages inspired and united his followers. From their loyalty and common purpose followed everything else: not just the territorial expansion from Catalonia to Hungary, or the revival of the imperial title, but the study and manuscript-copying at St-Benoît, and this small but perfect chapel for its abbot's country residence.

Inside, it is centred on a lantern tower, on a plan much like those of the squat little Byzantine churches which were going up at the same period in Greece and Calabria. Originally, like those, it had four equal apses round this tower. The west one, however, was pulled down later in the Middle Ages to make way for a nave. Byzantine influence is seen in the mosaic which fills the semi-circular vault above the altar apse. It shows in six rich colours the Ark of the Covenant, protected by four angels whom you would be less surprised to meet in Ravenna than beside the Loire.

Châteauneuf, back on the busy main road, is worth halting at in late spring for the display of rhododendrons in the park of its vanished château, and at all times for its *Musée de la Marine de Loire* showing the history of traffic on the river. But as soon as possible, cross back to the quieter bank, passing through Jargeau where Joan of Arc gained her first victory in open country after the relief of Orléans, and on through Sandillon for about a mile.

It is not easy to decide which track to take to the right towards the hamlet of Bagneaux. Fortunately two of them lead there, which at least increases one's chances. It is only on arrival outside the now empty farmhouse in the fields that an inscription on the wall tells us that it was once the home of the mother and the youngest brother of Joan of Arc. They came here in 1443, and worked for the reversal of the Church's sentence against her. This rehabilitation, the first stage in the process which led in 1920 to her canonisation, was proclaimed in their presence at Orléans in 1456. The mother, Isabelle Romée, died here thus reassured two years later. Her brother, Pierre du Lys, received a title.

Orléans, which lies straight ahead, has already been described. So cut across country to St Cyr-en-Val, in order to follow the

shortest river in France to have given its name to a *département*. The
Loiret rises in two distinct springs: one, a genuine fountain: the
other, a less dramatic welling-up. Both are in the grounds of the
seventeenth-century Château de la Source. The Tory chief minister
Bolingbroke spent here part of his exile from England after the
death of Queen Anne. He would approve of both uses to which his
old home has been put. The park containing the *source* itself has
been planted out as a *Parc Floral*. It combines a permanent shop
window for the seed and nursery industry for which Orléans is
famous, and an attraction for visitors. The château, on the other
hand, has become the administrative centre of the recently created
University of Orléans. *Restaurant universitaire*, residences, and
faculty buildings have arisen on the other side of the main road
among natural woods and a large man-made lake.

Those who wish to see the fountain of the *source* need not pay
the entry fee to the *Parc Floral*. It can be observed, free of charge,
from just at the back of the château. Purists might claim that it is
not the start of a real river, but is merely one of several *résurgences*
in this part of the valley. This means that it is a reappearance, after
some miles underground, of waters originating in the bed of the
Loire itself. If it is a fraud, it is hard to object to it. The Loiret's
eight miles of independence are a pleasure for any visitor, and most
of all for the *orléanais*. In and around the garden suburb of Olivet
they have established boathouses and restaurants at the water's edge,
and pleasant walks beside the old mills which the river used to turn.
Some of these have been turned into weekend homes.

When the Loiret joins – or rejoins – the Loire, which at Orléans
has touched its furthest point north, the road too bends south-west.
Soon a great Flamboyant Gothic structure appears, like a ship
becalmed on the water meadows, and then you are going down the
long wide street which is Cléry-St-André.

The first impression on entering the basilica is simply of the
space and sobriety so often associated with fifteenth-century
churches. And then you become aware, above eye level, of a figure
at prayer, with his back half-turned. It is the statue of Louis XI,
kneeling on top of his tomb and gazing towards the image of Our
Lady of Cléry. He had vowed to rebuild her sanctuary when
besieging the English in Dieppe in 1443. And here, loyal to the
Loire beside which he had spent so much of his life, he chose to
be buried. Michel Bourdin's statue of 1622, replacing the original

lost in the Wars of Religion, is true to its spirit, for although Louis XI may have been the most Machiavellian of monarchs, he was a wholly mediaeval man; and one of his daughters was canonised as Sainte Jeanne de France.

The suffix is to distinguish her from the other Sainte Jeanne. Joan of Arc may have been *la belle lorraine* by birth, but she too, like her Dauphin and his son, became *ligérienne* (of the Loire) by adoption. She has her own association with Cléry, through her companion Dunois, who contributed to its reconstruction, and was buried in a chapel on the right of the nave.

Three miles across the water meadows and over the river on a suspension bridge take you into Meung-sur-Loire. Although the church of St-Liphard is described as early thirteenth century, the impression it gives is overwhelmingly Romanesque. The château behind, built at the same period, was remodelled and extended in the eighteenth century by the bishops of Orléans, whose country residence it was. François Villon was imprisoned there, but an earlier poet with local associations was Jehan de Meung, who was responsible for much of the later part of the *Roman de la Rose*.

At Meung there are the first vines since Sancerre. Another locally-born poet, Jules Lemaître, has these reassuring lines on their effect:

> *Le petit vin de chez nous*
> *Est chose légère.*
> *J'en avale de grands coups,*
> *Il ne grise guère.*
> *Il me fait, quand je le bois,*
> *Le coeur et l'esprit plus droits.*

With its old streets made more picturesque by a winding stream called the Mauve, and its shady Mail*, this is also the first of the many charming little market towns on the lower Loire. In fact I prefer Meung to Beaugency, the next, slightly larger and better known place along the right bank. The name has a fashionable ring about it, one that appeals to tent or furniture manufacturers when they are wondering what to call a new model. It even had the right

---

* This word, which has given our 'Mall', and hence Pall Mall, originally meant a wooden mallet, and was then applied to the promenade along which a game using the *mail* was played.

sophisticated sound for Ian Fleming, when his James Bond was
wondering where to take a girl friend on holiday.

There really is plenty of interest to see as one threads one's way
through the mass of visitors. It was in the first place a monastery
town, and in the much restored Romanesque abbey church of
Notre-Dame were held two provincial Councils. The other monastic
buildings, which occupy the foreground of the view of Beaugency
from its fine, partly Renaissance bridge, were rebuilt in the eighteenth century. Rising behind them is the eleventh-century keep of
the castle, the rest of which was built four hundred years later by
Dunois. It shelters a regional museum. Among many mediaeval
and sixteenth-century houses there is a Renaissance town hall.

Between Beaugency and Blois the main road is not only very
busy, but quite a distance from the river. Those with plenty of time
may therefore find it well spent in meandering along the sideroads
to the left, which serve quiet villages with carefully maintained
houses and gardens. Especially attractive is Cour-sur-Loire, with
its church and modest château standing back from a spring on the
very bank of the Loire. This is dedicated to Ste Radegonde, the
Frankist princess who was a favourite saint of the early Middle Ages.

There is nothing modest about the château whose terraced gardens
run right down to the water's edge at Ménars. It is unusual, in this
land of the mediaeval and the Renaissance, in belonging mainly to
the eighteenth century. Kings had then long since left the Loire, and
few country houses were going up outside the Île de France, where
they were within reach of Versailles. But the woman who bought
and transformed it in 1760 was very much of Versailles, and very
closely associated with the King. She was Madame de Pompadour,
and her taste is still reflected in the wings and pavilions designed by
Gabriel, and in the gallery and orangery of Soufflot. Nor is it
shamed by the furniture of the period placed in them by the great
industrial company which now owns the château, even if some of
it is Louis XVI.

From Blois it is necessary to make a detour south of the river to
see some of the most memorable châteaux of the region. They stand
on the edge of the mournful Sologne; and it may be asked why they
were sited here, when the pleasant Loire was so near. The answer
was *la chasse*, still the principal *solognote* industry, despite all the
heath and marsh that has disappeared under cultivation since
Napoleon III founded his model farm at Lamotte-Beuvron. And it

is still one of the most popular occupations of Frenchmen, despite the competition from sport and television. The temptation of this game-infested countryside was even greater when there was so little else to do with one's time. Fortunately, too, the best hunting country of all lay on its western edge, within relatively easy reach of the Loire and Cher. There, as you could see on the horizon from the bishop's garden at Blois, lie the great forests where deer and wild boar feel most at home.

None of these 'hunting lodges on a grand scale' is more closely surrounded by the forest than the biggest of all of them: Chambord. It can be reached either by a pleasant run up the left bank opposite the gardens of Ménars, and then inland; or directly across country. Both routes for the last couple of miles run through the immense forested National Game Reserve.

The château itself stands in a clearing, vast enough to form a worthy stage for the departures and returns of the royal hunt. In numbers and degree of organisation this was something between a full *corps de ballet* and a regiment. But today the attraction is not here, but the place where the more distinguished part of the audience used to gather.

The roof of Chambord, a terrace from which rise elaborate chimneys, dormers and turrets, has been likened to a village in the skies. It gave the members of the court as many 'props' for dramatic entrances, tête-à-têtes, and other forms of intrigue as any palace or garden. Contrasting with the lack of decoration of the walls below, it symbolises the supreme flowering of the earlier French Renaissance. Yet it is hard to say whether it was deliberately planned; or whether it simply grew, until the effect it gave was recognised and developed. No one knows who was the architect, or even if there was a single architect. It is probable that French builders were responsible for the general plan, and Italians for the details. François I himself took an overriding interest from 1519 on, when he decided to extend the hunting lodge of the Counts of Blois which had long stood there.

The general plan is conventional enough. A rectangle with four round corner towers surrounds a keep. The keep forms part of one of the sides, and is itself surrounded by four more round towers. It differs little from the plan of many later fifteenth-century *châteaux-forts* except in its size. But none of these ever had anything resembling the *grand escalier*, or the magnificent lantern tower which crowns it.

This mysterious double staircase, which enables two people to ascend or descend without ever meeting each other, fascinates all who see it. It perhaps reflects that hidden side of the nature of François I which the painter Clouet saw behind his eyes, and which is hinted at again in his personal device, the salamander, which appears in the ceilings of the surrounding guardrooms, and on the lantern tower.

The history of Chambord did not end when François transferred his building instincts to Fontainebleau, or when royalty deserted the Loire altogether at the end of the century. Henri II completed much of his father's work. Louis XIV often stayed here and watched Molière as an alternative to hunting (Molière's peasants speak with the accent of the Orléanais). Louis XV's father-in-law King Stanislas of Poland and the Maréchal de Saxe spent long periods here. In 1821 it was purchased by national subscription for a baby a few months old: Henri V.

His story often confuses people, not least because he appears in history under three different names. His father, the Duke of Berry, was the second son of the prince who in 1824 succeeded to the throne as Charles X. This Duke of Berry was assassinated in 1820, leaving his beautiful twenty-two-year-old widow pregnant. It can therefore be understood why a million and a half francs were raised when she gave birth to a posthumous son, the Duke of Bordeaux. It can also be understood why this son often preferred to use the title of Count of Chambord, as an acknowledgement of such generosity. And when this young man's grandfather Charles X died in exile, and his father's elder brother died childless, it was he who became the legitimist pretender as Henri V.

His chances of succession were very high in the years immediately after the Franco-Prussian War. Bonapartism was discredited; the Third Republic was hardly established. The United States and Switzerland were the only other republics in the world of any significance. Nearly two-thirds of the Parliamentary deputies were in favour of a monarchy. So was Maréchal Mac-Mahon, the President of the Republic.

But Henri V, a Bourbon to the core, refused to accept the Republican *tricolore* as the flag beneath which he might have ruled over a united nation. The Restoration was so near a thing that the carriages which would have taken him and his entourage to a triumphal entry into Paris are still shown to visitors. When he died in 1883 his line died with him. He left Chambord neither to his

Orléanist rivals (of whom the Count of Paris is the present representative), nor to the people of France who had bought it for him, but to a junior branch of his family, the Bourbon-Parmas. The state was able to acquire it after the Bourbon-Parmas fought for the enemies of France during the First World War.

The visitor may leave Chambord with any republican sympathies he may have mildly reinforced. The château itself is so massive, the forest so vast, and the hamlet for the guides and gamekeepers so isolated, that its possession by a single family, even though they were mostly absent, would make life claustrophobic. For once, the change from *domestique* into *fonctionnaire* has had a humanising effect.

So overwhelming is Chambord that some of the châteaux of the neighbourhood, though great houses in their own right, seem no more than its lodges. They were built by royal servants: Herbault, seven miles south-east, by the *maître d'hôtel* of François I; Villesavin, six miles south, by his *secrétaire des finances* while he was in charge of the construction of Chambord (which may have inspired his own charming roofline); Neauregard, eleven miles south-west, by a *secrétaire d'État* of Henri II. This last has a seventeenth-century gallery of historical portraits. The style of all three is still essentially Renaissance.

On the other hand Cheverny, ten miles south, although it must also have had much of this style when it was the home of Raoul Hurault, *secrétaire* of Louis XII, and his son, the *chancelier* of Henri III and Henri IV, was transformed by his grandson in 1634. In its gleaming white stone exterior, and in its sumptuously panelled and painted rooms, it has all the qualities of the age of Louis XIII. French taste had gained symmetry and balance, without losing the energy and imagination of the previous century. Much of the beautiful furniture is from the later reigns of Louis XIV and Louis XV. A pleasant feeling of continuity about the whole is due to the fact that the owners are still Huraults (after a gap when Cheverny was in other hands during the eighteenth century). But here the château, although it dominates, does not crush the village at its gates. In the parish church with its wooden porch the members of the family are buried. Like their royal masters, they were, and still are, devoted to *la chasse*. There is a museum in the stables of their hunt and some of the prize specimens of game it has taken.

While Cheverny is post-Renaissance, two other châteaux of the region: Le Moulin, twenty miles south-east, and Fougères, seven miles south-west, are just – but only just – pre-Renaissance. Despite the towers and moat of the first, and the keep and fortifications of the second, there are too many windows and too much decoration for these late fifteenth-century residences to be *châteaux-forts*, the working fortresses needed when the Hundred Years War was still raging.

From Fougères it is only a six-mile cross-country run back to the Loire at Chaumont. Here a better known château hovers between Middle Ages and Renaissance, but in a different way. Chaumont was built as a square, but in two stages. Two wings went up between 1465 and 1481 simply as a fortress, but the defensive character of the two later wings which rose between 1498 and 1510 was masked by decoration. Among the most interesting of the monograms to be observed as one crosses the drawbridge are a volcano (hot mountain, *chaud mont*) and the 'D' of Diane de Poitiers. The castle was forced on her in exchange for Chenonceaux by Catherine de Médicis, the vengeful widow of her royal lover.

The entrance between two corner towers brings an unexpected view. This is one case where an eighteenth-century demolition has done good. The destruction of the north wing – one of the two earlier ones – has opened up a magnificent view across the valley, and of the Loire itself at the foot of the hill.

It is therefore more pleasing today than in the time of the two rival women who in turn owned it. We are shown their bedrooms, with furniture of their period. Catherine de Médicis' spirit seems most present here, just as Diane's is at Chenonceaux. The elaborate nineteenth-century stables in a corner of the park – closed for repair on my last visit – were built by the husband of one of the more recent owners.

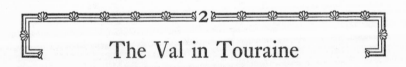

2
The Val in Touraine

The road along the left bank is pretty and quiet as it leads into Touraine. But there is much to be said for crossing to the right bank, simply in order to approach Amboise from across the river.

The bridge straddles the end of an island, where there is a street or two of old houses. A well equipped camp site upstream occupies the greater part of this Île d'Or – a name which suits it. There is a golden tinge to the memory of every visit I have made to Amboise. Perhaps it is due to the golden stone of the château and quays, to the sandy *plages*, to the setting sun on the wide river, or to the golden quality of any July day beside the Loire. Amboise, at the centre of the classic Loire circuit, is likely to prove the crowning point of many visits to the Valley.

High above the river and the town on a promontory of land, the château – once much larger than it is today – still shows on a grand scale the change of style of the late fifteenth century.

The exquisite chapel of St-Hubert, the two massive towers with their famous spiral ascents wide enough to take a rider on horse-back, and the royal apartments facing the Loire, were built by Charles VIII before his unsuccessful but culturally profitable Italian expedition. They therefore belong to the last fling of Flam-boyant Gothic. The wing of Louis XII behind, on the other hand, was only begun by him, and its upper storey was completed under François I during the flowering of the first French Renaissance.

That flowering centres on Amboise in a special sense. Not only did François I spend much of his early reign here before he had begun Chambord; it was also here that he brought the most complete Renaissance man of them all: Leonardo da Vinci. He gave Le Clos-Lucé, a manor less than half a mile away, to him in 1516, and Leonardo lived there until his death three years later. Built in 1471 of rose-red brick, with angles and windows in stone, it stands in a small wooded park. It is perhaps the most liveable-in of all the monuments along the river, more on a modern scale than the great châteaux, yet not as primitive as, say, Rabelais's La Devinière. It is suitably filled with furniture of the period, although only the frescoes of the chapel, the work of some of his students, were actually seen by him. In the basement are a number of modern models, constructed from his designs to prove that his ideas work.

It is interesting that besides acquiring his *Mona Lisa* and his *The Virgin, the child Jesus, and St Anne* for the Louvre, François I persuaded him to draw up plans for draining the Sologne, and for a canal to link the Loire with the Saône. But his one permanent legacy to the region is his bones, now in all probability in the chapel of St-Hubert.

On learning that the château is the private property of the Count of Paris, many people probably imagine, as I did, that it has in some way come down to him from the Valois, via the Bourbons. In fact it was bought from the crown just before the Revolution by the Duke of Penthièvre, and left by him to Louis-Philippe, the Count's ancestor.

The town of Amboise is interesting in its own right. The church of St-Denis is Romanesque. St-Florentin is late Gothic. The town hall is Renaissance. There are many sixteenth-century houses, one of which now houses a fascinating Museum of the Postal Service. It is also surrounded by some lovely country: the forest of Amboise in a wide semi-circle to the south, and beyond that the valley of the Cher.

The most direct road there across the forest passes after a couple of miles the short drive on the right to the Pagoda of Chanteloup. Near this in the eighteenth century stood a château, which was granted to the Duke of Choiseul, Pitt's opposite number during the Seven Years War. He extended it and made it the centre of a little realm which included Amboise, Chenonceaux and Montrichard. He retired here when forced into exile from Paris between 1770 and 1774. Just as the friendship of a king's mistress, Madame de Pompadour, had earned him these grants of property and his dominant position in the government, so the enmity of another, Madame du Barry, had caused his temporary disgrace. Cut off from the court, he gathered here a miniature Versailles of his own.

Part of the château's décor survives in the museum of Tours, but the brilliant society which gathered in it has left more permanent memories. Beaumarchais, for example, picked up here many of the details for his *Mariage de Figaro*, including the character of Chérubin, and even the name of the dog Linda. And at the end of his exile Choiseul built the pagoda – a more elegant version of the one which had gone up a decade earlier at Kew – in honour of the loyalty shown by his friends.

Chenonceaux, best-known of all the 'châteaux of the Loire', is in fact on the Cher and therefore belongs to books on this river. It is worth mentioning, though, that it also has literary associations. In 1747 Jean-Jacques Rousseau spent a happy time as tutor here. Exactly a century later Flaubert was a guest.

Rousseau's host and employer was a farmer-general of taxes; and the castle's builder more than two centuries earlier had been a receiver-general of finances, Thomas Bohier (other financiers of the period built Azay-le-Rideau, Beauregard and Cheverny). Yet like no other château, in its situation astride the Cher, in its quintessentially Renaissance architecture, and in the woman with whom it will always be linked, it makes us think of love and beauty.

When Diane de Poitiers lived here while her lover, Henri II, twenty years younger than herself, was king, the château lacked the two-storeyed gallery running out over the river, which is its best known feature. For that, and for all those Valois masques and fêtes whose shadows still people these woods, waters and formal gardens, thanks are due to Catherine de Médicis. The association of that sad woman with this region is deeper than generally imagined. Her father, Lorenzo, married her mother, Madeleine de la Tour d'Auvergne, in 1517 in Touraine. Henri IV's two visits to Chenonceaux, in 1598, were with the favourite of all his mistresses, Gabrielle d'Estrées. It was the death of this *belle tourangelle* in the following year, just when he was about to make her his Queen, which marked the end of the great age of the Loire Valley.

Eleven miles up the Cher a large but mysterious Roman building stands just outside the village of Thézée. More interesting for its age than its present appearance, it may have been a relay station of the imperial post, for changing horses and getting a night's rest.

Earlier guides do not mention Thézée, for it is only recently that it has been adopted by Maurice Druon. Now his series of novels, *Les rois maudits*, adapted for television, has been seen by British as well as French viewers. But when I heard that their author had succeeded André Malraux as Minister of Culture, I was glad not just because he was a successful populariser of early fourteenth-century history, but because he has rescued this remote Roman monument.

The little town five miles beyond Thézée is St Aignan, like a small-scale Amboise, with a Renaissance château high above the left bank of a smaller river, a largely Romanesque church, and an equally good camp site on an island opposite.

Just beyond the edge of the Loire valley region proper, on the Indre, reached across lightly-populated *gâtine*, stands the great Renaissance château of Valençay. Talleyrand bought it as a place of exile for the Spanish royal family between 1808 and 1814. Also nearby are Loches and its powerful castle, with its memories of Agnès Sorel, another local girl who found a king's favours. A still more remarkable royal romance culminated at the château of Candé, near Montbazon, where on June 3rd 1937, the Duke of Windsor married Wallis Simpson.

Agnès Sorel was perhaps born at Fromenteau-en-Brenne, in the curious region of La Brenne between the Indre and the Creuse. About half its area is covered by lakes, although they are little noticed in passing through. Its strange charm at evening has been described by Vidal de la Blanche: 'with the oblique rays with which are lit up these sleeping pools, this heather and gorse between the birches and the clumps of pine'.

Just to the north, Azay-le-Ferron, southernmost of all the 'châteaux of the Loire', includes architecture all the way from the fifteenth century up to 1926. It is furnished appropriately for its respective periods, and includes a museum of La Brenne.

Le Grand-Pressigny has a quite different museum in its medi-aeval and Renaissance château, showing the development of the flints for which it was the prehistoric centre of production (as described in the historical section).

Returning to Amboise, you should again cross to the right bank, not only for the views from the raised *levée* of the Loire, and in due course of the towers of Tours, but also to visit Vouvray. This is not so much a place to see as a taste to remember. Numerous producers there offer the opportunity of trying the most famous of all the Loire wines both in its still and its sparkling form, and of visiting their well stocked cellars.

Less well known are the remains of the great abbey of Mar-moutier (from *majorem monasterium*) on the outskirts of Tours. Its wealth was expressed in the saying

> *De quel côté que le vent vente*
> *Marmoutier a cens et rente.*

Founded by St Martin himself, the only parts to have survived since it was sold at the Revolution are a gateway, the fortified wall, and the lodging of the Grand Prior. In the tufa cliff behind are the indestructible caves hollowed out by the Dark Age hermits.

Keeping to the right bank, you leave on your left the eighteenth-century bridge into Tours you have already crossed many times. After about ten miles is the château of Luynes, standing back from the river. All that a French mediaeval castle ought to be, with its towers capped by pepper-pot roofs, it is still lived in by the family

from Luynes in Provence for whom the village's name was changed
by Louis XIII. Next to a side road at the back, which gives further
good views of the château, stand the remains of a Roman aqueduct.

A much more impressive Roman monument comes into view four
miles downstream. This seventy-foot brick tower rising on top of
the *coteau* seems at first sight as though it had been put up, if not
yesterday, at least in this century. Only when close does the patina
of the ancient patterned bricks become apparent. The purpose of
this 'pile' is uncertain, but similar geometric patterns reappear on
the early mediaeval abbey of Ligugé, south of Poitiers, just as patterns on the aqueduct of Luynes are found again on another early
mediaeval abbey, St-Philibert-de-Grand-Lieu south of Nantes.

A mile further on, the village of Cinq-Mars has a Romanesque
church, and what remains of the château dismantled by Richelieu
after he had executed the young Marquis of Cinq-Mars for
conspiracy.

Until now the route has been alongside the *varennes*, a long
peninsula barely a mile wide between Loire and Cher, where
market gardeners grow vegetables for the housewives of Tours. Now
the two rivers merge, and three miles further on is Langeais.

Right at the centre rises one of the half-dozen major châteaux of
the Loire. It is also one of the most satisfactory to visit – although
on busy days one runs the same risk, here as elsewhere, of being a
member of a packed throng shuttled swiftly from guide to guide.
The satisfaction comes first from its having been built all of a piece
about 1465, so that there is no need to make the effort – often
interesting but sometimes confusing – of distinguishing between
the styles of different wings. Second, it has remained intact and
unchanged, thanks to its occupation first by short-term royal
tenants, and then by absentee owners. Third, it was beautifully
furnished and decorated by its last owner, who bequeathed it to the
Institut de France. He not only assembled fifteenth- and sixteenth-
century tapestries, paintings, chests and so on from all over France;
he even had replacement floors and ironwork copied from suitable
models.

The relative comfort of the interior, without which all this would
seem out of place, contrasts with the grim towers and fortifications
of the outside. Its builder, Jean Bourré, was also responsible for
Le Plessis-Bourré, built when Brittany was an independent, poten-
tially threatening power, whose Dukes might one day lead an army

up the Loire Valley. It was assured that they never would when in 1491 the fourteen-year-old Duchess Anne of Brittany was married in a large room on the first floor to the twenty-year-old Charles VIII. One of the witnesses was the Duke of Orléans, who three years previously had been her father's ally against her young husband. When that husband died it was he who was to divorce that husband's sister in order to make her for a second time Queen of France.

The present château marks an important stage in the conflict between the Valois and their vassals, while its predecessor stood in the Plantagenets' front line against the Capetians. Built by an early member of their dynasty, Foulques Nerra, before the year 1000, the ruins of its keep still stand on a hillock at the back of the château, and are said to be the oldest in France.

The house opposite the entry to the château may or may not have been, as claimed, once the home of Rabelais. What is certain is that it serves excellent *pâtisseries*; Langeais has always catered for the sweet tooth. It once owed its prosperity to its *sucrins*, the delight of Parisians, and in gratitude placed three of these sugared melons on its coat of arms.

There are two pleasant roads onwards to the north of the Loire. One follows the right bank of the river. The other, beyond the little Authion, which runs parallel in the valley almost all the way to Angers, links the string of wine-producing villages along the *coteau* where the valley at last rises. Bourgueil is the best known of them, and has given its name to the fine red wine for which they are famous.

The next châteaux, however, are across the river from Langeais. Turning left, in five miles you reach Villandry, on the Cher just before it joins the Loire. Like Herbault and Villesavin, this was built by a minister of François I. But the symmetry of its façades, and the lack of exuberance in its roofline, show that the underlying classicism of the French temperament was already taming the Renaissance.

The classicism is shown in the gardens, which extend on three terraced levels. On the lowest, the *potager*, nine square beds are cunningly filled with vegetables whose growth and flowering provide unexpected colour. On the level above them box hedges are arranged in arabesques of geometric hearts. Higher still, and further from the château, a classical garden centres on a lake in the shape of a Louis XV mirror. Finally, a lime-tree avenue separates the three gardens from an orchard running up the hill. But the scene which faced Dr Carvallo when he bought Villandry early in this century was quite different. Hills and valleys, groves of trees and winding paths formed a landscaped *English* garden deliberately built on top of the patient reconstruction we see today. Here, if ever, is your opportunity to acquire a taste for, or at least to appreciate, the formal *jardin français*.

The château contains Dr Carvallo's art collection, which is especially rich in the Spanish school.

The *caves* in the *coteau* bordering the Cher upstream at Savonnières are well suited for mushroom growing, and can be visited. But then you have to turn back and retrace the few miles which separate the Cher from the Loire's next tributary, the Indre.

This is an even gentler stream than the Cher, often hidden from the roads which follow it by the poplars which in recent years have been planted in the water meadows. There is something gentler, even, about Azay-le-Rideau, the Indre's water château which was built at the same time as Chenonceaux. Although early Renaissance in date, it curiously combines a superficially Gothic appearance with a symmetry of line which only became general much later. It takes its name from a thirteenth-century owner, Hugues Ridel. Again, it really belongs to the Indre rather than the Loire.

At Saché, four miles upstream, a *Musée Balzac* has been installed in the sixteenth- and seventeenth-century château. The creator of *La Comédie Humaine* was a guest for months at a time over many years, and worked on many of his books here. *Le Lys dans la Vallée* is set in this part of the Indre valley.

I have often spent a happy time in La Sablonnière just across the valley, tasting the good wines of Azay-le-Rideau in a friend's cool *cave*. More than once I have had a leisurely picnic on the hillside behind, where the American sculptor, the late Alexander Calder, had set up his vast metal mobiles. Painted in strong primary colours, they move in the wind or at the touch of a firm hand. Surprisingly they add to, rather than disturb the peace of the classic *tourangeau* countryside below. And the white-haired artist himself, driving out at the wheel of his Citroën, used to seem completely at home. His works were not permanent features. On my last visit an impish red devil revolved in the place of a more abstract mobile which had been bought by a wealthy museum or municipality.

I also remember the land to the south of the Indre, the *gâtine* which separates it from the next valley south, that of the Vienne: camping beside the isolated ruins of the Renaissance church of Les Roches-Tranchelion; and discussing at sunset with a farmer under forty, how in his childhood he had a dozen neighbouring children to play with. Now there were only two of school age.

There are other, more remote memories here too: Charles Martel's victory in 732 on the Landes du Ruchard, and the possible Arab ancestry of the people of the Véron. This, the largest of all the low-lying, fertile *varennes*, occupies the tip of land between Vienne and Loire to the west of the vast forest of Chinon. Now it has suffered an even more alien visitation: the nuclear generating station of Avoine. Its huge white spheres make us wonder at first whether Martians, instead of simply Moslems, have settled beside the Loire.

There are memories and to spare at Chinon, a charming little town beneath a long hill covered by a ruined *château-fort*.

Chinon, petite ville, grand renom.

It was in that Plantagenet fortress that Henry II died, defeated by Philippe-August and deserted by his sons. Two hundred and fifty years later the Valois Charles VII, 'roi de Chinon' even more than 'roi de Bourges', received there at his dynasty's weakest moment the recognition and the help of the unknown Maid from Lorraine. Pierre Levéel writes that the Anglo-Angevin Empire died in the château of Chinon, and that Valois France was reborn there. In the town below, François Rabelais, whose father was a lawyer here, spent much of his childhood.

Chinon, and the Vienne valley as a whole, are covered in other books, but I will just mention one town in this area: Richelieu. Built by the great Cardinal as a model town at the gates of his now demolished château, 'it witnesses to the reasoned, if not the reasonable fantasy of the greatest minister of old France'. The older houses of the *pays* of the Richelais are still covered by the round red tiles of Aquitaine instead of by the slates of Anjou, recalling that before the Revolution it was attached to Poitou.

Those tiles can be seen by travellers on the little *belle époque* train which puffs all summer between Richelieu and Chinon. It is run by a French railway conservation society. When I was at Richelieu station one cool September evening the season had already ended, and I was surprised to find the firemen stoking up.

I was still more surprised to see the platform filling with men in frock coats and women in long dresses. They might have stepped straight from the Third Republic of Sadi Carnot or of Monsieur de Fallières, but they were very solid ghosts. On questioning, they explained that this was an unusual wedding reception for two of the keener amateur railway enthusiasts. The Vouvray corks were popping in the brightly lit dining car as they steamed away into the night towards Chinon.

Although it is a little outside my territory, I feel bound to take you from Chinon across the Vienne and out towards La Devinière, for Rabelais, who was born here, is with Descartes and Péguy the presiding genius of the whole region.

Somewhere between a small manor and a comfortable farm, the stone building with outside staircase, standing at the end of a short cul-de-sac, is in reality a late fifteenth-century *résidence secondaire*. This was where the family came for supplies of fresh food, to enjoy the grape harvest, or simply to get away from town. Just as some of the best childhood memories are not of one's own home, but of visits to a schoolfriend, or of holidays with an aunt in the country, so it seems here that the young François remembered most fondly.

This greatest prose writer of his age travelled so much in later life that he hardly ever returned here. But a short stay in 1532 in what he called his '*pays de vache*', at the moment of the *vendanges*, set his imagination alight.

Pantagruel was already almost complete. The following year *Gargantua*, too, was finished. His whole childhood is there relived 'in memories scarcely veiled, but enlarged out of all proportion: the family home, the adjoining field and the ford over the stream, the relatives and the friends, the quarrels with the neighbours, the pastry-cook Innocent and the 'painted cave' (which still exists at Chinon), the pancake-makers of Lerné or the Sybille of Panzault...' There is still no more certain way of getting the feel of Rabelais' work than to wander round the streets of Chinon or to walk, book in hand, from La Devinière to Lerné, across vineyards or beside lanes lined with willows and walnut trees.

As you explore the scenes of the Picrocholine War, or Seuilly, where Rabelais went to school at the monastery, you will find an almost fairy-tale castle on a *coteau* to the south. It is the château of Coudray-Montpensier, which already dominated the landscape in the time of Maître François.

Earlier in this century it was bought and restored by the Flemish writer Maurice Maeterlinck. It is a tribute to the inspiration to be had from this superficially unexciting countryside that it had such attraction for the creator of *l'Oiseau bleu* and of *Pelléas et Mélisande*. If Rabelais himself read this he would no doubt laugh, and attribute its inspirational qualities to something very much closer to its soil: to the wine of Chinon, or to that strong red wine with a slight taste of violets called *le breton vermeil*,

> *qui poinct ne croist en Bretaigne,*
> *mais en ce bon pays de Verron.*

This *bon pays de Verron* includes Ussé, which stands about the same distance to the west of Langeais as does Villandry to the east. The two châteaux both have terraced grounds descending to the level of the river. In both cases the river – the Indre at Ussé, the Cher at Villandry – runs parallel to and only a short distance from the Loire itself. Ussé on its *coteau* looks out over the double valley formed by the convergence of *fleuve* and *rivière*. One of the best places from which to capture the charm of Ussé – pepper-pot towers and decorative fortifications against a background of 'tufted trees' – is from the *levée* along the left bank of the Loire itself, half a mile away.

The mystery given by a little distance is perhaps necessary to appreciate why this was probably the model for Perrault's castle of the Sleeping Beauty. The quality is due again to the late fifteenth-century contrast between a fortified mediaeval form and an elegant Renaissance execution. The builders in this case were the Bueils, one of the principal *tourangeau* families on the French side in the Hundred Years War. A detailed visit reveals the work of later centuries: the sixteenth with the exquisite chapel, which stands by itself and has fine carved stalls and Aubusson tapestries telling the life of Joan of Arc; the seventeenth in the main staircase; and the eighteenth in the *chambre de roi*.

No sooner has the Indre finally met the Loire than they are joined by another and greater affluent, bigger than any since the Allier. The Vienne has itself already been enlarged by the Creuse. Its confluences at Candes, at the southernmost point of the Loire below Orléans, forms one of the classic landscapes of the region. Behind a shifting sandbank of a promontory lie a couple of islands, then scattered woods, and finally the distant *coteaux*.

It is a suitable landscape with which to remember *le jardin de la France*. Its foreground is occupied by the last village in Touraine, Candes itself. Its fortified church stands on the site of the house where the greatest *tourangeau*, St Martin, died after being taken ill on a journey in 397.

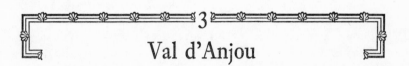

3
Val d'Anjou

Only a mile downstream into Anjou lies Montsoreau, with a château giving straight on the road. As one would expect from its date of 1455, it is still mainly a fortress. It now serves as a museum for Lyautey's Moroccan campaigns, and for the local soldiers he recruited there, the fierce Goums.

The burial place of the greatest Angevins, Henry II and Richard Coeur de Lion, lies only three miles to the south, at the very edge of their native county. The importance of the great abbey of Fontevrault is outlined in the historical section. Here an abbess ruled a double community which included both convent and monastery. Apart from the great domed church – just too early to be Angevin in style – there are cloisters, a chapter house, and a noble kitchen not unlike a later Byzantine church.

The road on from Montsoreau runs beneath a *coteau* on which, just after Souzay, stands a manor house with its own interest for English visitors. The Plantagenets were not the last Angevins to reign across the Channel. In 1445 the daughter of Le roi René married young Henry VI.

It is hard to see the cherished princess of the peace-loving, cultured court of Angers in the fierce, power-seeking Queen Margaret of Shakespeare and of historical tradition, the terror of the Yorkists and the one royal figure before whom the Kingmaker at last knelt. But her passions were those of a wife and mother rather than political. When her own son was murdered after Tewkesbury, and her husband after Barnet, she retired quietly to end her days here above the Loire in 1482.

You will get the most out of this approach to Saumur if you know the miniature showing what it looked like in the fifteenth century in the *Très Riches Heures du Duc de Berry*. Even now, the view of it is the same, complete with the vineyards almost up to the entrance to the grounds, which produce the sparkling white wine for which the Saumurois is famous.

But it would no longer serve as model for the Castle of Love of Le roi René, who wrote: '*Et pour plus proprement le donner à entendre le dit beau chastel était de façon telle comme celui de Saumur en Anjou qui est assis sur la rivière de Loire.*' Although the tall, white building with its elegant towers remains the same, the gilded weathercocks which crowned the pepper-pot roofs, and the decorative crenellations and slim turrets which surrounded them have disappeared. The simple palisade which separated pleasure garden from vineyard has been replaced by fortifications almost like those of Vauban. In fact they belong to two or three generations earlier than Vauban, when Saumur was the Protestant stronghold on the Loire, and Duplessis-Mornay, the Governor installed there by Henri IV, was anxious from the first that the château should work as a real castle.

Next, this 'Pope of the Huguenots', as his enemies called him, founded in 1599 an academy which made Saumur the intellectual capital of Protestant France. Inevitably the town lost a large part of its population at the revocation of the Edict of Nantes.

A century later an academy of a different kind arose when the crack cavalry regiment of the Royal Army was stationed here. The most glorious moment of the Cavalry, and later Armoured Corps School, came on June 19th and 20th 1940, when its pupils, with heavy loss of life, held the Loire against the panzers.

It remains the biggest institution in Saumur, its white buildings and stables occupying much of the west of the town. The huge open square of la Carrière is still the scene late in July of brilliant exercises by the '*Cadre Noir*', the Black Squadron of riding instructors, though most of the training nowadays is inevitably in mechanised warfare. The traditions of the School are also seen in the château, the upper floor of which has become a *Musée du Cheval*. Besides skeletons of famous race-horses, and Stubbs prints, it includes collections of bridles, saddles, and spurs, and a library.

On the floor beneath the *Musée des Arts décoratifs* has fine French ceramics, small sculptures, and Limoges enamels. The loveliest and oldest of these is a crucifix as old as, and like that from the tomb of Geoffrey Plantagenet at Le Mans.

The town has a small late Gothic town hall, and two Romanesque churches with many tapestries. Its most unlikely monument is the classical Notre-Dame des Ardilliers beside the Loire, which has a separate, domed rotunda. Like Château-la-Vallière thirty miles away across the river and the *gâtine*, this has associations with a discarded mistress of Louis XIV, in this case Madame de Montespan, who halted on her way to visit her sister the Abbess of Fontevrault. Her spiritual director was head of the community for which the church was built, and she herself gave one of its altars.

Like Amboise, Saumur has a 'suburb' on an island in the river; and islands, though mostly uninhabited, become more frequent on the way down the Loire. Meanwhile the chalk *coteaux* with their wine cellars hollowed out of the tufa continue. One village is even named Chênehutte-les-Tuffeaux.

It is immediately followed by Trèves, where a low Romanesque church surrounded by cypresses crouches beneath a hundred-foot keep of the fifteenth century. Out of proportion, yet curiously balanced, they seem lost beneath the immense sky of the Loire.

It is less than a mile to Cunault. The church of the monastery which once stood here would have disappeared with it had it not been for Prosper Mérimée, who by combining the professions of literature and of *inspecteur des monuments historiques* is rather like his contemporary Anthony Trollope at the British Post Office. He saved a superb Romanesque unity, not really broken by the Angevin vaulting of half the nave. The long time it took to build, of which this is evidence, means that the many carved capitals tell a great deal about the development of sculpture from the late eleventh to the early thirteenth century – as well as much about twelfth-century daily life. There are some fragmentary frescoes, and, rarer, a thirteenth-century shrine in painted carved wood.

Yet the most abiding memory of Cunault is the first: the view looking in at the door, down two hundred and forty feet of gradually narrowing nave, unchecked by any transept. The perspective effect is increased by the steps at the entrance to the choir, and by the fact that height is slightly greater than breadth.

The pretty village of Gennes, a mile and a half on, has two largely Romanesque churches. One, of which the nave is in ruins, is at a superb viewpoint, which is also the fitting site of a memorial to the

Cadets of the Saumur School of Cavalry, who died defending this countryside. In the foreground of this view, just across the Loire at the end of a long suspension bridge, lies Les Rosiers. Although I feel it improper to name or recommend any individual hotel or restaurant, there are here two excellent, if expensive, establishments, where the *cuisine ligérienne* is judged by many to attain its ultimate.

From Gennes the main road cuts across country away from the Loire, and you must take a narrow side road beside the river to reach the unimpressive, but beautifully situated remains of the once famous abbey of St-Maur. The seventeenth-century buildings, with a single gable surviving from the abbey's great days in the Carolingian world, were occupied on my visit by young people on holiday from all over France and abroad. On a level above stands a twelfth-century chapel, claimed to be the furthest point to the west reached by Joan of Arc on her journey.

It is near the end of the long necklace. There is only one more important château on this side of the Loire. But Brissac is special: it is still owned and lived in by the Dukes of Brissac, descendants of the Marshal of France to whom Henri IV gave a million and a half *livres* for negotiating the surrender of Paris. This enabled him to enlarge and transform his family fortress, of which two round towers can still be seen.

It also enabled him to employ numerous artists, carving outside and painting within. This rich decoration in pilaster and painted ceiling gives a lingering air of the Renaissance to a building constructed between 1614 and 1621, which is added to by the prevailing sixteenth-century style of furnishing and tapestries. Nowhere does one feel more of what a living château must have been like in the great age of the Loire Valley.

On the other side of the river, to which the little Authion still runs parallel in their joint, wide valley, three more châteaux stand not far from Angers. Montgeoffroy, off the 'inner road' from Bourgueil, was built like Brissac for a Marshal of France, and is likewise still lived in by his family. But the Maréchal de Contades started work on it in 1775, so that it is a rare thing in the Loire valley, a château of the reign of Louis XVI, when most such building was confined to the region round Paris.

Rarer still, every piece of its furniture, made and signed by the great cabinetmakers of the day – and this was the same time as when Hepplewhite and Sheraton were working in England – has never been moved from the place for which it was ordered and designed. A long-absent owner, returning at the end of the last century, was able to check the inventory drawn up for the Marshal when he took possession. It would still serve today.

Much nearer Angers along the same road, out of sight of but not far from the slate quarries of Trélazé which roof *l'Ouest*, stands another château of the same rare period. Pignerolles is a deliberate copy of the Petit Trianon, but after serving as the headquarters of Admiral Doenitz during the last War, it holds no original furniture.

Serrant is ten miles the other side of Angers, on the rather dull main road to Nantes. As at Brissac and Le Lude, its builders had to adapt classical ideas to an already existing fortress. They managed to remain notably true to the original Renaissance concept, though their work went on until the beginning of the eighteenth century. The original plan was by Philibert Delorme, architect of the Tuileries and of Fontainebleau.

Perhaps to strengthen this link with royal palaces, it is claimed that the chapel was designed by Hardouin-Mansart, the architect of Versailles. It shelters an imposing tomb by that sculptor of *le grand siècle*, Coysevox. There is a certain overall royal air about this westernmost *château de la Loire*, which gave hospitality both to Louis XIV and to Napoleon I.

Though all the major châteaux are now behind, there remain over thirty miles of the river itself before it enters Brittany.

The first place of interest after St Maur is Les-Ponts-de-Cé, one long street of two miles interrupted by no less than seven bridges across the Authion, the Louet, a canal, and the various streams of the main river. This important crossing-place has been the scene of military engagements during practically every war from Caesar's *Bellum Gallicum* to the Liberation of 1944. It is the last place where the Loire can be crossed before it is swelled by the Maine, itself enlarged by three major and a dozen minor *rivières*. It also marks the limit of *la vallée angevine*, the fertile stretch between Candes and Les Ponts-de-Cé, widened by the Authion, which even that *tourangeau* chauvinist, Pierre Levéel, considers as much *le jardin de la France* as Touraine itself.

Downstream the valley narrows between steep slopes, so much so that part of the road long the left bank has been called *la corniche angevine*. Farther down, at Champtoceaux, it practically forms a gorge.

Yet the essential spirit of the Loire Valley continues right to the Breton border. As R. Dion puts it: 'Descending this happy flow, where scenes of rural wealth follow each other, one fails to notice that one is penetrating little by little into *l'Ouest de la France* ... Between the wild *bocage* of the Mauges and of the Segréen, it is a whiff of the air of Touraine which is carried down as far as the lower Loire.'

The 'air of Touraine', as Rabelais would have understood it, smells of grapes. The picturesque island of Béhuard, with a quaint fifteenth-century chapel where pilgrims still come to an ancient statue of the Virgin, may mark where the Loire leaves behind sand and chalk to force its way through the granite of Armorica. But the vineyards go on, not only along the *corniche angevine* itself between Rochefort and Chalonnes, but on the equally steep slopes of the little tributary, the Layon. The *coteaux du Layon* give the finest wine of Anjou, a great, mellow white wine obtained from the over-ripening of the grapes called *pourriture noble*. Six *communes* which devote themselves almost exclusively to this, and which produce particularly good wines, are allowed the special *appellation* of *Coteaux du Layon-Villages*.

Two of the vintage wines of Anjou are from this restricted region: Bonnezeaux, from a mere 300 acres; and Quarts de Chaume from only a third this area. The latter lies in the territory of Rochefort-sur-Loire, and derives its name from the quarter of the vintage once reserved for the *seigneur*. The third vintage wine comes from around Savennières, just across the Loire and opposite the island of Béhuard. Its church, perhaps the oldest in Anjou, dates in part from as early as the ninth century.

Although the Savennières vintage grapes are grown in a restricted area of 150 acres, these spread along the steep hillsides for several miles. One such vineyard has the lovely name of Coulée de Serrant. Right in its centre stand the ruins of the keep of La-Roche-aux-Moines. Destroyed in one of the obscurer incidents of the Wars of Religion, it had earlier been the scene of a far more important battle. In 1214 King John had at last organised his revenge on the rival who had deprived him of his Angevin inheritance. As ally he had the Emperor of Germany, who was to attack by the classic German invasion route from Flanders. John meanwhile was to invade his family lands, where he might expect support.

Their plan of dividing the French forces was successful, but nothing else was. Philip Augustus marched north to crush the Emperor and his allies at Bouvines on July 27th. However he had no need to return to support his son, Prince Louis, whom he had sent against John. Louis had already come upon the Plantagenet army besieging La-Roche-aux-Moines. In defeating them on July 2nd he had made certain that the river would remain the royal Loire.

This would be a suitable point to end, if there were not a more suitable point still in the very last Angevin village on the river. Liré was the birthplace of the poet who proudly signed himself 'I.D.B.A.': Joachim du Bellay, Angevin. In a magical poem written when homesick in Rome he has immortalised the slate (*l'ardoise*) of Anjou, and has plucked the one word which more than four centuries later still expresses the charm, the graciousness, the mildness, the essential '*douceur*' of the whole 'Loyre' Valley.

> *Quand revoiray je, helas! de mon petit village*
> *Fumer la cheminée, et en quelle saison*
> *Revoiray je le clos de ma pauvre maison,*
> *Qui m'est une province, et beaucoup d'avantage?*
> *Plus me plaist le sejour qu'ont basty mes ayeulx,*
> *Que des palais Romains le front audacieux,*
> *Plus que le marbre dur me plaist l'ardoise fine,*
> *Plus mon Loyre gaulois que le Tybre latin,*
> *Plus mon petit Lyré que le mont Palatin,*
> *Et, plus que l'air marin la douceur angevine.*

Appendices

I

Getting There

The approaches to the Loire Valley by road are fully covered earlier in this book. Those in a desperate hurry, and who are prepared to pay the tolls, can also speed to Tours or Le Mans along newly built motorways.

Main railway lines follow the routes we described as the Nationale Sept, 'the Capetian lifeline', and 'the Maine road'. From Orléans a line follows the right bank of the river all the way to Nantes, although the *rapides* from Paris to Nantes run more directly through Le Mans and Angers. As mentioned, the building of the trunk line to Brittany through Le Mans and Laval has been responsible for a loosening of the traditional bonds between Maine and Anjou.

The occasional *autorail* still provides the leisurely tourist with views of unspoilt countryside on the branch lines from Chartres to Saumur through Château-du-Loir, and from Paris to Tours through Châteaudun and Vendôme.

One of the most enterprising and successful small airlines in Europe, Air Touraine, now operates both scheduled and chartered flights between Tours and Britain. From the pleasant little airport of Tours, four miles out on the N 10 to Paris, there are also regular flights to several other French cities.

II

Maps

Michelin sections 59, 60, 63, 64, 65, 67.
Shell 'Cartoguides' No. 6: Val de Loire, and No. 7: Centre.

III

Practical Details

The French Government Tourist Office, 178 Piccadilly, London
WIV OAL, supplies list of hotels and other brochures, including
the invaluable *Val de Loire – pays des châteaux*, which gives opening
times and entrance fees of châteaux, abbeys and museums, churches
of architectural interest, and details of *Son et Lumière* performances,
exhibitions and festivals. The FGTO generally has available the
excellent brochures produced by the departmental *Comités du
Tourisme*, such as *La Mayenne*, describing every village in the
department, or *Anjou: meublés, locations, vacances, gîtes,* which each
year lists furnished accommodation available in Maine-et-Loire.
If not, they can be acquired direct from the Syndicats d'Initiative
of the departmental capitals.

IV

Climate

The weather of the region, subject to almost as many influences as
that of Britain, cannot be pinned down by hard and fast rules. But
my own personal experience over a number of years is that visits
before May 15th are often blighted by cold spells, and that those
after September 10th are sometimes ruined by rain.

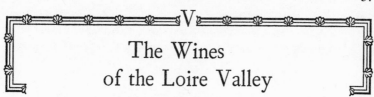

The Wines
of the Loire Valley

by

George Mortimer

The range of high-quality wines produced in the Loire Valley is so vast that it is difficult to do much more in the limited space here than briefly catalogue their names, and in some cases give an indication of their quality and taste.

To avoid repetition, *appellation contrôlée* wines are indicated at first mention with an asterisk * and VDQS (*vins délimités de qualité supérieure*) with a dagger †. Beside these wines you will meet innumerable *vins de table* at much lower prices. You will be glad to hear that many of these will be of a quality superior to similar simple wines found elsewhere in France.

The vineyards extend almost to the sea; starting from the mouth of the river, Paimboeuf, almost on the Atlantic just across the river from St Nazaire, is right in the Muscadet country. This white wine is to most people in this country *the* wine from the Loire Valley (though some might also claim this for Anjou rosé). There are three separate *appellations*: Muscadet Sèvre & Maine*, Muscadet Coteaux de Loire*, and Muscadet*. The first of these is the one most commonly seen in the United Kingdom; its area of production as the name implies is between the *rivières* Sèvre and Maine before they join the Loire at Nantes. Muscadet Coteaux de Loire is produced between Nantes and Ancenis. Muscadet Coteaux de Loire and Muscadet are almost all consumed locally – though sometimes one does meet the latter in this country, and it is often slightly cheaper than Muscadet Sèvre & Maine.

Muscadet should be drunk young; as a counsel of perfection, in the year following the vintage. It is a dry, fruity wine with a well balanced, well developed bouquet. Perfect with fish and shellfish, as is right for a wine produced so close to the sea, it is also very suitable as an apéritif. (At the risk of seeming disloyal to Burgundy,

I have found that Muscadet mixed with cassis produces a delicious *Kir*.) In view of the great commercial success Muscadet is enjoying at the moment in this country it is amusing to reflect that it was for a great many years considered to be a wine 'that could not travel'.

Most Muscadet producers also grow the lesser white, Gros Plant, or, to give it its full title, Gros Plant du Pays Nantais†. Gros Plant is a light, dry, acid wine superb with oysters; the producers are still apt to shake their heads in wonder that their extra dry 'little' wine suits the *goût anglais*!

Both Muscadet and Gros Plant sometimes indicate on their label that they have been bottled *sur lie*. This means that the wine has been bottled by siphoning from the top of the barrel so that the lees are not stirred up; this avoids disturbing the wine by racking it, and helps preserve its freshness, bouquet and finesse.

Just before Angers, there is produced Coteaux d'Ancenis Gamay†, the first (geographically) of the many rosé wines produced in the valley. Made from the Gamay grape, it is light and dry; worth sampling locally, as I have never seen it available in this country. Moving into the heart of the valley around Angers, the famous wine names become more frequent. First, three rosés: Rosé de Loire* (dry), Rosé d'Anjou* (demi-sec) and Cabernet d'Anjou* (sweet). A chilled bottle of vin rosé is so delectable to weary tourists that it is well worth remembering which of these three *appellations* is the one you prefer.

Then there are the luscious, rich, sweet whites of the Coteaux du Layon*, crowned with the estates of Bonnezeaux* and Quarts de Chaume*; the two latter, in great years, challenging Yquem itself 'without its cloyingness' (or, at least, that is what the producers say). Other separate *appellations* of rich wines in the Coteaux du Layon are the communes of Coteaux du Layon Chaume*, St Lambert-du-Lattay*, St Aubin-de-Luigne*, Rabley-Rochefort*, and Beaulieu-Faye-d'Anjou*. All well worth sampling *in situ*. Pleasant medium-dry white wines are sold under the *appellations* of Anjou*, Coteaux de l'Aubance*, Coteaux de Saumur*, and Anjou Coteaux de la Loire*.

There are four *appellations* of red wine produced around Angers: Anjou*, Anjou-Gamay*, Saumur* and Saumur-Champigny*. The last named is sold extensively in Great Britain and is claimed to be the most northerly *appellation contrôlée* red wine produced in

France. With the exception of the Gamay, all these reds are made from the Cabernet-Pineau d'Aunis grape. In good years the wines are fruity and *velouté*, but, of course, being grown so far to the north, there does come the occasional summer when the wine can be a little acid. Ask to taste before purchasing; vintage charts are most unfair to individual producers. Good wine is made somewhere every year, since some vineyards enjoy favourable 'micro-climates'. Yet if a *vigneron* uses great skill and labour to make fine wines in an 'off' year it is most certain that he will not get a good price for it, so cautious are buyers. All producers, and often restaurants, bars and some shops in France, will offer a taste before purchasing.

To conclude this section of the centre of the valley, Saumur* is a dry white wine (a blend of Chardonnay and Sauvignon grapes), Savennières* is another dry white, but with an extraordinary 'nose' of such richness that one thinks that the wine must be rich and luscious. It is a tribute to the producers that even after sniffing this, one is not disappointed to discover that the wine is in fact dry.

Finally, the sparkling wines. Saumur has some of the largest producers making these wines in what must be the most natural factories in the world – caves cut deep in the chalky rocks close to the Loire and Cher. These can be visited, and a tour around the labyrinthine passages in the cliffs, with hundreds of thousands of bottles at every stage of maturity, and finally a glassful of wine makes a delectable afternoon. This is especially so if the sun is very hot. But take warm clothes – these cellars are very cold. Ackerman-Lauvance and Bouvet-Ladubay are two large companies who welcome visitors.

The production of sparkling wines in the Loire valley is very scattered. Saumur*, Touraine*, Montlouis*, Vouvray* and Anjou rosé* are the usual *appellations*. There are many producers, ranging from the large firms at Saumur and Vouvray to small concerns operating on almost a cottage industry scale. The wines are made in the same way as is Champagne, and the grapes are grown on the same type of soil, but the price is considerably lower.

The next section of this journey upriver leads to Touraine, with Tours at the centre. Here there is a thick cluster of great red wines: Chinon*, Bourgueil* and St Nicholas de Bourgueil*. Made from the Breton (Cabernet franc) grape, these wines may not nowadays be made exactly as they were in the time of Rabelais, but this does not stop the proud locals from pointing out the many references in his books to these wines. All these reds are fruity, with a marked bouquet; one French author has ascribed to them 'an aroma of raspberries, wild strawberries or violets, depending upon the exact spot on which the grapes were grown'. If you are disappointed in not discovering these elusive aromas, take heart. I have been in the wine trade for more than 30 years and I, too, am still searching. Not that anybody needs any extra reason for drinking these wines. They are particularly good for summer drinking, and – unusually but most importantly – should always be served like the Gamay wines of the Loire, quite cool, at cellar temperature.

This is also the area of the Touraine Gamay*, which is increasingly imported into this country as the price of Beaujolais rises more and more. Made from the same grape, it can be almost exactly like it, and in no sense an inferior substitute.

Vouvray* and what used to be called the poor man's substitute for it, Montlouis* (grown on opposing banks) are both wines which are only harvested when the grapes have reached the stage of over-ripeness known as *pourriture noble*. On the little *rivière* Loir is the small *appellation* Jasnières*, which makes similar wines.

Touraine Sauvignon* is a delicious dry white, full of flavour and with a flowery bouquet. I should not be surprised if its popularity were one day to eclipse that of Muscadet. There is a rarity which I have not tasted, Chinon *blanc**, nor have I tried Amboise *blanc**, or the rosé produced at Touraine-Mesland*. However I have tasted, and can heartily recommend, Amboise rosé* (which is dry) and the superb dry aromatic white wine from Azay-le-Rideau*; I write 'dry' but in fact the *appellation* produces a glorious rich wine in a fine year, and a *sec* in other years.

Finally, moving up the valley one comes to the wines of Sancerre* and Pouilly Blanc Fumé*. Both these wines, although considerably more expensive than Muscadet or Touraine Sauvignon, are very popular in Great Britain, and so I need only draw attention to Sancerre Rouge* and Sancerre Rosé*, neither of which is commonly available in this country. Pouilly Blanc Fumé, (not to be confused with the Pouilly Fuissé of Burgundy), should equally be distinguished from its neighbour Pouilly* simple, a pleasant enough wine but not of the same quality (nor, in fairness, price). Quincy* (made exclusively from the Sauvignon grape) is a fine, and I think underappreciated, wine. The red, rosé and white wines produced at St-Pourçain-sur-Sioule†, like those of Menetou-Salon* and

Reuilly*, can only easily be purchased locally; but being able to buy reasonably priced local wines of such high quality is part of the charm of visiting the Loire valley. If you like a light Sancerre, try the white Reuilly or Menetou-Salon.

Bibliography

The two essential guide books are the green Michelin *Châteaux de la Loire* and the Guide Bleu *Val de Loire*. Michelin, as always, offers its illustrated information in more accessible but shorter form. Its English edition, unfortunately, keeps very close to the river itself, leaving out the hinterland which the Guide Bleu covers in full detail.

There is the same contrast between the two series which examine aspects of the region in greater depth. The Larousse *Découvrir la France* series (e.g. *Le Maine et la Normandie*) is attractively presented and very up to date, yet scholarly in its judgements. Horizons de France in 1968 brought out a new edition of their more academic *Visages de la France* series under the general title *Les nouvelles provinciales*. The region, previously divided between four volumes, is now covered by one on Maine and Anjou, and another on the Orléanais and Touraine.

Of the provincial histories in the *Que sais-je?* series issued by Presses Universitaires de France, the best is Pierre Levéel's *Histoire de la Touraine*.

Index